A
YEAR
FOR
YOU

Also by Stephanie Bennett Vogt
Books in the Spacious Way Series

Your Spacious Self: Clear the Clutter
and Discover Who You Are

A Year to Clear: A Daily Guide to
Creating Spaciousness in Your Home and Heart

A YEAR FOR YOU

Release the Clutter, Reduce the Stress, Reclaim Your Life

STEPHANIE BENNETT VOGT

Hierophant publishing

Cover design by Emma Smith
Cover art by PlusOne | Shutterstock
Interior design by Frame25 Productions

Hierophant Publishing
www.hierophantpublishing.com

If you are unable to order this book from your local bookseller,
you may order directly from the publisher.

Library of Congress Control Number: 2019943384

ISBN: 978-1-938289-91-0

Printed on acid-free paper in the United States.

To my readers and students
whose stories inspire me every day.

Your clearing is my clearing.

CONTENTS

INTRODUCTION

If you get the inside right,
the outside will fall into place.
—Eckhart Tolle

Some of you may be thinking, *A year? You've got to be kidding. I'm already overwhelmed . . . My piles are insane . . . I have no time to take my time . . . I need answers and solutions now!*

While a year commitment may seem long, or daunting, or even onerous, let's look at it in a different way. A lot can happen in a year. Especially a conscious year spent consistently doing something that you love, need, and want to cultivate in your life.

The truth is, most people rarely set out, purposefully, to spend 365 days doing something nourishing—something just for themselves—with a commitment to mark the changes that arise in their lives. We don't know how powerful we can be, transforming our lives, taking care of ourselves, one day at a time over an extended period of time.

Well, I do. I have lived it myself, and I've watched tens of thousands of readers and students live it too. They've journeyed with my book *A Year to Clear* and my 365-day course on DailyOM called *A Year to Clear What's Holding You Back!* I've read thousands of Facebook posts and DailyOM comment threads from people just like you reporting personal transformations like these:

> I cried this morning as I read the final lesson as I don't want it to end. This has been more than just a study course for me. It has become a friend, a mentor, a guide, an ally. A supportive, loving, grounding voice that reached out to me through the miracle of a smartphone. I am profoundly grateful to have found this gem on that Christmas Eve one year ago, when I was depressed and hopeless and lost. My heart is full of gratitude for this gift.

> What a year! I came into the course feeling overwhelmed by the mess in the basement, the mess in my studio, the mess in my drawers, the mess in my closet, and the mess in my head. During the year, I slowly and drippingly accomplished so much clearing! My studio is now functional, my kitchen is neat, my bed is made every day. I meditate regularly, am in the process of organizing a lifetime of my old artwork, have found much better communication and more mutual compassion in my marriage, and (I don't want to forget this part) I adore my relatively empty closet with its wardrobe of comfortable clothes and accessories I love. And best of all, my head is so much more clear. Thank you, Stephanie

Bennett Vogt and *A Year to Clear*. Here's a salute to the amazing possibility for growth and renewal that exists in the human soul!

Day 365 . . . I did it!!!!! I wondered, Would I stick with it? Would I feel different? Would the shifts be noticeable? Yes. Yes. And yes. I have been able to experience the subtle shifts that were promised, and without even noticing I have opened, and flowered, and am definitely at peace. Thank you, thank you!!! Stick with it. At times the slow drip is uncomfortable and/or seems like nothing is happening. Have faith. From deep below, great change is occurring.

Now whenever my husband finds me tearing up at my computer, he knows I'm reading comment threads. These brave adventurers may start slow, but believe me, they pick up steam! A year has legs and staying power. It *never* gets old watching the Spacious Way work its magic. I love witnessing people experience the simple wonders of going slow and celebrating the humbling beauty of letting go.

And as if the personal transformation in these community forums weren't enough, I marvel at the ability of these adventurers to move each other. Their stories of triumph and challenge often read like poetry and inspire an extraordinary outpouring of support and compassion. The clearing journey transforms us and, in so doing, transforms others as well.

If a year seems too long, consider that it's taken far longer than a year to build up the stressful patterns that afflict us all on a regular basis. Stress—and stuff—doesn't grow overnight, and releasing it takes time. It takes time to rewire a brain that instantly goes into fight-or-flight. It takes time to soften resistances to new ways of being. It takes time to grow new habits that feel really good and create lasting change. Taking one year to gently tend to our physical, mental, and emotional well-being is a small price to pay for what we gain in return. Even if all we can handle is just one conscious minute a day, the nourishing benefits are beyond measure.

Yes, I'm talking about a journey and a way of life, not just a destination with a set goal and outcome. And unless we go on the journey and stick with it, we cannot fully know what our higher self wants to teach us.

Why stop short when we can go so much further into game-changing territory?

Play the big game. Play the long game. Commit to yourself for a year, and see what happens. All you have to do is say *Yes!* and take the first step.

The Spacious Way

When I began my career as a space clearing practitioner and teacher in 1996, I was troubled by the growing epidemic of stress and stuff that has become the reality in our culture and our world. With all the resources and support available to us, I wondered why most clearing methods, though well intentioned, were falling short of helping people clear for good. Why did they always feel so tedious, onerous, and joyless? Why didn't they last?

It took me twenty years to break the code: to answer those questions, field-test them, and develop a whole new method that can address an epidemic that could bury us alive.

The result is the Spacious Way: a conscious distillation of space clearing, modern science, mindfulness, and *kaizen*: the Japanese concept of small steps leading to big changes through continuous improvement. Blended together, they work to release physical, mental, emotional, and energetic clutter—from the inside out.

Instead of "attacking" the stress, "getting rid" of the stuff, and "overcoming" the overwhelm, as most methods teach, the Spacious Way works more gently to release the underlying causes—the patterns, resistances, and attachments—of anything that holds us back. One minute of "slow drip" clearing morphs into more minutes, less effort, and less baggage. It promotes a calmer nervous system, a quieter mind, more ease, more space, more light, more joy.

The Spacious Way changes the paradigm from effort to ease. It offers a whole new way to clear that is simple, feels good, and lasts.

And yes, it's a game changer.

Foundation, Journey, Practice

What you are holding in your hand is the third book in my Spacious Way series. (Don't worry, you do not need to have read the first two to gain the full value of this one.)

For those of you familiar with my work, you might be interested to know how this book relates to the others in the series. Here's how they stack up, as it were:

◇ *Your Spacious Self* is the foundation for a whole new simpler way to clear. It gives you the concepts, science, and practical tools behind my proven "slow drip" method of clearing anything that holds you back.

◇ *A Year to Clear* is the journey. It applies the principles from the first book and walks with you every day for an entire year as you peel away the layers of stress and stuff and ease into new ways of being.

◇ *A Year for You* is the practice. It takes you deeper into the clearing journey by focusing on the five actionable steps to spaciousness (aka, the five S's): slowing down, simplifying, sensing, surrendering, and self-care. You'll discover that steeping in this process for a full year is not a diet, it's a feast!

While each book informs and supports the others, each stands on its own. They can be read in any order, separately or at the same time. Some readers are drawn to the foundation and choose to start there. Some are drawn to the journey and choose to start there. Some are drawn to the practice and choose to start there. Together, they gently help you experience more of who you are, in ways that are easy, fun, and lasting.

As I've said many times (and will repeat until the end of time), cultivating a spacious way of life is a journey that never ends and gets better with time. Each book will work its magic on you no matter where you choose to start.

What to Expect

This book is comprised of fifty-two chapters, or lessons, designed to be read, cultivated, and experienced slowly, one week at a time. The lessons are divided into six segments, as follows:

◇ Weeks 1–10: Slowing Down

◇ Weeks 11–20: Simplifying

◇ Weeks 21–30: Sensing

◇ Weeks 31–40: Surrendering

◇ Weeks 41–50: Self-Care

◇ Weeks 51–52: Coming Home

Each chapter opens with a quotation to connect you to the theme and spirit of the lesson. From there you'll be guided to the heart of the lesson via an inspirational story, teaching, and/ or tool designed to deepen your experience of one of the five steps to spaciousness (the five S's). The chapter closes with an invitation to apply the material in two ways: a Practice that gives you one to three action steps to adopt during the week and a series of open-ended writing prompts called Journal Revealings for further contemplation in your journal.

You'll find that the weekly chapters start slow and build upon one another. By the time you reach the surrendering stage beginning in Week 31, you will better understand how this five-part process fits together. You'll also be more prepared to navigate the bumpier waters of this work as you strengthen your spacious muscle and go deeper into "letting go" territory.

While it is conceivable to complete the weekly lessons more quickly, I don't recommend it. The real goodies, as explained earlier, are in the daily practice. Slow down, and enjoy the journey.

You see, the more you repeat a practice, the deeper you go. The deeper you go, the clearer you get. The clearer you get, the more spacious you feel.

Sound good?

How to Use This Book

The following guidelines will help you gain the most from your yearlong experience. Please read them carefully and take them to heart:

> **Focus on one week at a time**: Choose a quiet moment and location to read the lesson—preferably on the same day and in the same place each week. Read the message at least twice: once to get the overview and general vibe and once to go deeper. Sometimes it helps to reread the message from the previous week before opening and integrating a new one.

Practice daily: While each lesson is designed to be read once a week (see above), the Practice action steps at the end of each chapter are designed to be repeated *every day* for seven days.

Be open: Enter into each week with an open mind. Suspend judgment and be willing to not know. You may be pleasantly surprised. If a message mystifies you, just be with that.

Trust the process: If it feels like some lessons or practices are shorter than others, it's because they are. This helps you benefit more readily from their invitations to slow down and simplify. Some weeks will be longer and richer. Trust the process.

Stop and feel: The daily contemplations, inspirations, and practices will open you up to new information that may not be familiar or feel comfortable. Bring as much beginner's mind to them as you can.

Don't identify: If a lesson presses a button or kicks up some emotional weather, consider it an opportunity to bring compassionate awareness to it and yourself. It's likely a sign of stuck energies that are coming to light to be loved and healed from your past, from other people, and/or from your living spaces. It's all good. Unpleasant sensations usually pass to the degree that you don't make them "yours."

Allow silence: Silence creates openings and opportunities to feel. Don't fear it.

Have fun! Don't take yourself or anything that happens too seriously. Being less attached to an outcome will raise your energy level, expand your perspective, and lighten your load.

If, at any point, you start to get off track, lose steam, or feel edgy and resistant, it could be a sign that you're bumping up against an old pattern, a stuckness, a fear. Congratulations! There is great learning right at hand for you. Breathe into it. Review these guidelines to help you come back to center. Refocus, recommit to yourself, and return to the practice.

Practices

For the Spacious Way to work its magic, you need to supply two things: awareness and consistency. You cannot achieve any level of deep, sustainable clearing results without them. By awareness, I mean bringing all of your attention to a task and allowing thoughts and feelings to arise without doing anything to fix, change, or manage them. And by consistency, I mean doing this work on a daily basis.

So how do we get better at being aware and consistent in our efforts when we lose focus, get stuck, or fall off the wagon? That's where practice comes in. The practices that accompany each weekly lesson are specifically designed to help you soften resistance, build your awareness skills, and grow new habits that lead to consistent action. Practice every day, even for just one minute, and your life will change.

They say that practice makes perfect. While that may be true in some instances, this motto does not help us here. If anything, it will hold us back. What *is* helpful is this simple reframe: "practice makes spacious." Adopt it as your new mantra. It will serve you well.

You see, when it comes to clearing the Spacious Way—where the focus is on softening and releasing old patterning (instead of striving for and becoming attached to outcomes)—perfection is not our friend. Let that one go right now. Next time the old perfectionistic voices start harping again, remember your new mantra and reach for a practice instead.

Journal Revealings

Clearing, by definition, is about shining the light of awareness and compassion on patterns that we have kept locked up in darkness for a long time, maybe even our entire lives. It is also about shining light on anything new that wants to come through and get our attention.

The open-ended journal prompts that close each lesson are designed to help you do that—to help you name, examine, love, heal, off-gas, embrace, explore, and/or otherwise shine light on your experience. Whatever comes up for you this year—whether it illuminates or exasperates—is what I call "revealings." A journal is a perfect place to contain them.

For that reason I invite you to get yourself a blank book, notebook, or journal. Use it to reflect on your daily practices and record any shifts, aha moments, dreams, synchronicities—anything that shines light on your experience. Highlight your most inspiring entries to come back to when your intentions start to flag, you get derailed, or you lose focus.

If you use your journal as it is intended, it could be your best friend and confidant this year.

Raising the Game

A final word about clutter and clearing before we get started.

While many of the lessons in this book focus on your home and possessions, you will not be getting a how-to tutorial on organizing them. Marie Kondo and FlyLady.net are much better suited for that. What you will get from me instead is an opportunity to take your clearing to a deeper level: to peel away the layers of stress and stuff that may have caused your home and your life to get so out of balance in the first place.

Clearing is an inside job that begins and ends with you. As you will soon discover, clutter as we know it—the piles in our house, the noise in our head, the pain in our heart—is ultimately *not* the problem. It is the pathway, the solution—a symptom of something deeper that will be revealed and healed (to the degree that we are ready and willing to meet it).

Clutter is your teacher. Make friends with it. It will show you the way.

All right, then. Let's play!

PART 1

SLOWING DOWN

*What you cannot see in this world is far more powerful than
what you can see ... what is under the ground creates what is
above the ground ... what is invisible creates what is visible.*
—T. Harv Eker

Perhaps you're wondering, How can we slow down when everything in our world is about progress and speed? And why would
we even want to slow down when it might be so much more fun
to travel in the fast lane?

Here's what I can tell you: So much is lost when we move at
hyperspeed. We cannot make vital connections. We cannot see
what is holding us back. We cannot hear what our heart wants
to tell us.

If we can't see it and feel it, we can't clear and heal it.

The moment we start slowing down—on purpose and with
purpose—is the moment things start to open up and change.

So kick off your shoes and get comfortable. We're going to take a nice long ride in the slow lane. You may just discover one of the Spacious Way's best secrets: the less you rush, the easier it is to let go . . .

and flow . . .

and grow.

WEEK 1

Take Five

It so often happens that somebody says "change your life" and you repaint your car rather than re-wire the engine.
—Pico Iyer

We've all had those days. Days where we've poured our heart and soul into doing something that matters, doing the work of becoming ourselves, and then it gets hard.

We lose heart. We back off. We bail on ourselves.

In one of his posts, blogger and thought leader Seth Godin calls it "transformation tourism":

I bought the diet book, but ate my usual foods.

I filled the prescription, but didn't take the meds.

I took the course . . . well, I watched the videos . . . but I didn't do the exercises in writing.

> Merely looking at something almost never causes change. Tourism is fun, but rarely transformative.
>
> If it were easy, you would have already achieved the change you seek.
>
> Change comes from new habits, from acting as if, from experiencing the inevitable discomfort of becoming.

Mr. Godin is right, of course. And I would add one caveat to his message: the work you do to become yourself may not be easy, but it doesn't have to be hard, either. It can be soft. It can be gentle. It can be slow.

Daily repetition, conscious baby steps, and compassionate self-care are potent habit changers.

So is beginner's mind. There's a powerful magic that happens when you suspend judgment and enter into an experience with the innocent curiosity of a child. The less you know, or think you know, the more spacious and revealing it is.

If you're wondering how you too can cultivate beginner's mind and grow a daily practice that you love, is sustainable, and leads to spacious revelings, let's just say that you have the keys already. Below I'll show you what they are, and what they might open up for you when you use them this year.

Five Steps to Spaciousness

Built into the lessons of this book are five keys, or steps, that are at the heart of this journey. Together they work to replace effort with ease, clutter with clarity, drama with dreams.

I call them the five steps to spaciousness (or the five S's for short). Here's what they are and what you'll receive when you spend ten weeks with each step:

Slowing down: The first S is all about cultivating ease. You'll notice what happens to old habits and overwhelm, limiting thoughts, and resisting patterns when you stop rushing and make time for what matters.

Simplifying: With the second S you'll experience how the biggest changes come from taking the smallest steps. You'll connect with your best teacher—your home—as a pathway to lighten your life. You'll discover that when you consciously tend to your home every day, you are tending to yourself. There is no separation.

Sensing: The third S gives you an opportunity to tune in to, and fine-tune, your six senses (smell, taste, touch, hearing, seeing, and inner knowing) as a way to experience the transformative effects of energy, light, and beauty that abound. You'll discover that there are no mistakes when you follow your "knows."

Surrendering: The fourth S helps you step back and become bigger than any challenge, pain, or wound that may be holding you back. You'll learn that it's not about giving up, as many of us believe, but rather a conscious and powerful way of stepping up (your game) by stepping back.

Self-Care: The fifth S is not only about making time for yourself, feeling good, and putting the "spa" in spacious. It's also a revolutionary act that can change how you relate to everything.

Though the steps are presented one at a time in a particular order, ultimately it is through consistent application and integration of all five steps that you'll start to enjoy the magic benefits. Each stage naturally builds upon the others to shift the way you act, think, and feel—for good!

Overwhelmed? Excited? Curious? Mystified?

Congratulations! You're right where you should be.

Begin now with slowing down and taking some time to reflect on this gift of a year you have given yourself.

Practice

Why do you think it's necessary to rush? What would happen if you slowed down even just a tiny bit? What are you looking forward to most about this year?

The practice this week is twofold.

1. **Observe:** Every day this week, practice slowing down. Notice the ways you run through your day on autopilot. Take five minutes longer to empty the dishwasher, for example. Or give yourself five extra minutes to enjoy your morning coffee. If you tend to speed on the highway, drive a bit slower

(safely, of course): move into the slow lane and go the speed limit.

2. **Look forward**: Write a letter to your future self following the steps below.

Looking Forward Process

Set aside at least fifteen minutes and find a quiet and comfortable place to sit. Take a few swigs of water, and have a separate piece of paper and pen handy (not your journal). Read everything through before you begin.

Step 1: In a two-part letter to your future self . . .

◇ Describe the reality that you are living today. Reflect on how you feel in this moment and what motivated you to give yourself a year for you. Be as specific as you can.

◇ Describe the reality that you hope to be living in a year from now. Envision how clearing your life will pave the way for miracles.

Step 2: When you feel complete . . .

◇ Sign the letter, date it, and place it in an envelope.

◇ Seal the envelope and on the front write: "Open on Week 50."

◇ Store the envelope in a safe place where you'll remember to find it.

◇ Reflect on your experience in your journal.

Journal Revealings

Deepen your experience of this lesson by completing the open-ended phrases that follow. They are deceptively simple, designed to bypass the thinking mind and release buried insights and unprocessed clutter. Don't think too hard or force the answer. Allow your highest wisdom to reveal itself in these responses and all subsequent journal explorations from here on:

◇ Tasks or pleasures I can extend by five minutes every day this week . . .

◇ What it feels like to write to my future self and name what I am ready to release . . .

◇ What it feels like to name and claim what I most wish to manifest this year . . .

WEEK 2

Ease and Breeze

Life opens up when you do.
—Crest Toothpaste Ad

On a bright and promising January 1, my husband and I took a sabbatical. We left our home in Concord, Massachusetts, to spend six months in the mystical, magical town of San Miguel de Allende, Mexico.

We rented out our home, downloaded some books on tape, and drove 3,000 miles to our new residence south of the border, a place where we could dial it (way) down and watch what happens when we unplug from life as usual.

And what a big reveal it was! From boot camp opportunities in letting go to mind-bending encounters with nature, beauty, and art, the days were as diverse and varied as the cloud formations were at sunset.

In those six months we guzzled enough sunshine to last another ten years. We witnessed up close the murmurations of birds and watched our flower garden go from zero to exuberant. We met Yann Martel (*Life of Pi*) and watched master poet David Whyte lift an entire audience with his mesmerizing wordplay at the San Miguel Writers' Conference. We walked the mineral-paved roads of the sixteenth-century ghost town Pozos and got naturally high on the energies there.

We steeped in the melodies played live on a 1720 Stradivarius (aka "the Red Violin") and listened to Latin jazz in an old hacienda with twenty-foot ceilings. We hung out with old friends and made new ones. We engaged in a favorite ritual of waving goodnight to the sun as it eased like clockwork below the horizon. We called it "the show," and we made it a habit never to miss it.

We had some days with no internet and some with no electricity (which also means no internet). Some days seemed to go on forever, and others passed in the blink of an eye. Such was life in the slow lane that half year.

And every day since.

None of these things would have happened if we hadn't left the comfort of our home and taken the challenge to invite more wonder and mystery in our lives. That experience was a game changer.

But if you're thinking you have to take six months and move away to some foreign land to have your mind bent in a million different ways, think again. If you can find a way to dial it down a notch, tune in to what's hiding in plain sight, and let go of attachment to the outcome, I would wager that you too will have some pretty jaw-dropping experiences of your own, wherever you are.

There is a magic that happens when you deliver continuous nourishment to your body, mind, and spirit every week for a whole year; a lightness when you embrace the discomfort of not knowing what's going to happen next; a freedom when you adopt daily practices in slowing down, simplifying, sensing, surrendering, and self-care.

As Wayne Dyer once said, "When you change the way you look at things, the things you look at change." And change they will—in the best ways possible.

So imagine that this is Day One of your sabbatical and you are packing for the journey. You'll need to bring some supplies to remind you of home. What do you need to support you? And where would be a good place to put them?

Gathering a few things that you love into a special dedicated space in your home is a good way to start your adventure. You can think of it as a symbolic collecting of all the scattered parts of yourself. Like a personal altar to yourself, or a focal point, you can use this dedicated space to quiet the mind and anchor your intentions for the upcoming year. Use it to read your weekly lessons and journal. It can be your home base anytime you need help staying grounded or just getting some peace and rest.

What happens when we go off road into new territory is that our old homing tendencies have a funny way of wanting to redirect into old, comfortable, not-helpful ways of being. An anchoring altar is a great way to bring you back to your center.

Practice

What does it feel like to gather yourself in an intentional way? What does it feel like to gather yourself in a sacred way?

To help you find out, I invite you to use this week to create an anchoring altar by following the steps below.

Creating an Anchoring Altar

1. **Identify**: Find a room, corner, nook, bookcase . . . any place that is yours only (i.e., that's off-limits to family members, housemates, coworkers, pets, etc.) that can serve as your home base this year. If space or

privacy is an issue, use a lockable drawer, a suitcase that you pull out from under the bed, or a lockbox.

2. **Gather**: Beginning with a good pen and an empty notebook or journal, gather a few essentials for your journey: favorite books, poems, photos, a candle, incense . . . anything that helps you feel at home with yourself. If it's a place where you can retreat for a while, you might include a comfy chair, a basket with a cozy blanket, art supplies, soothing music, a yoga mat, a meditation cushion . . . whatever feels good and nourishing.

3. **Place**: Once you've identified a spot and gathered a few of your favorite things, take a little time to *consciously* arrange your objects in a way that feels good. Note: This step doesn't have to be a huge production. One or two things placed with awareness and love are sufficient.

4. **Connect**: Close your eyes, light a candle, and clarify your intentions for the year that you wrote about last week. Tune in to your feelings of excitement and any apprehensions you may be feeling. If it helps and resonates, you can include other forms of artistic expression, like collage or drawing, to deepen your experience.

5. **Refresh**: Keep your altar fresh and vibrant by replacing objects regularly. Move your altar to another location (or remove it altogether) if it isn't working for you.

Journal Revealings

Like you did with Week 1, complete the open-ended prompts to deepen your experience of this week's lesson and practice:

⋄ Objects that make me feel grounded, centered, and excited about the coming year . . .

⋄ Intentions for my journey . . .

⋄ Worries for my journey . . .

⋄ What it feels like to gather myself in a more conscious and intentional way . . .

WEEK 3

No Rush

You can't force a rosebud to blossom
by beating it with a hammer.
—Rachel Naomi Remen, MD

In our home in Mexico we had a bougainvillea varietal that had no blooms. No matter what I did (new pot, more sun, gentle whispering), it just wouldn't budge—until this year, when we returned in the winter to see a joyful exuberance of color.

Some things just can't be rushed.

There's a saying about the planting cycle of a new garden: the first year the plants sleep, the second year they creep, the third year they leap.

I like to think that cycles like these pertain to us too as they relate to waking up to, and becoming, more of ourselves—more of who we are meant to be.

When I quit a twenty-year career as a high school Spanish teacher back in 1996, I had no idea that the next big chapter in my professional life would take another twenty years. There was nothing cluing me in that I would go on a deep dive into a whole new field of study, personal clearing, teaching, and writing to fully live and embody the work I came here to do.

Teaching I could understand. But writing? Publishing multiple books? *Seriously?* I was a slow reader in grammar school. I spent my summers in high school getting tutored in writing. There was nothing on my radar that even hinted at the idea of becoming an author.

You could say that most of my professional life has been one of "sleeping" and "creeping" before I could finally begin leaping. The running joke in my household is that it's taken me forty years to become an overnight success.

And still, knowing all that—knowing how long it would take to fully come to understand and claim my true purpose— I'm grateful for all of it. Even when it didn't look like much on paper, took decades to come together, and often made no practical sense from a financial standpoint, all of it mattered. Every slow, obscure, messy, exasperating step I took informed my journey. And, thankfully, despite the many bumps, the twists and turns, the delays and disappointments, I stayed with it.

That said, while the plant cycle appears to stop at "leap," we all know that the story doesn't end there. There is no end point to "becoming." Just like a plant, there are periods of expansion and periods of contraction for humans too. There are growing periods and resting periods, shedding periods and blooming periods. As long as the roots are well grounded, nourished, and fed, there is no end to our growth cycle. My "true purpose" will, no doubt, continue to unfold and illuminate. Who knows where my journey will take me next and what it will uncover? What I do know is this: We do not need to "bloom" in order to blossom.

What would blossoming in your life look like? Would you be willing to wait days, months, even years, if necessary, if you knew that's how long it would take for a higher dream to blossom in your life? What wants to reveal itself to you now?

These are what I call wonder questions—questions that are not meant to be answered in the traditional, linear way. They invite you to contemplate them, savor them, live them.

Like I say, some things just can't be rushed.

Practice

When it comes to self-realization, where do you think you are in the cycle of sleep, creep, leap? Would it be okay with you if it took some time for you to blossom?

Use this week to reflect on the wonder questions of this lesson in your journal, or choose others that may have come up as a result of writing down your intentions in Week 1 or anchoring them in Week 2. Notice the little blossoms and glimmers of light that are beginning to reveal themselves since you began working with this book.

Journal Revealings

⬦ I am at the _____ stage of my sleep/creep/leap cycle, and this makes me feel . . .

⬦ If I took the time to allow it to happen, blossoming in my life might look and feel like . . .

⬦ What is wanting to reveal itself to me now is . . .

⬦ Shifts and insights that are bubbling up for me already since I began three weeks ago are . . .

WEEK 4

Go Slow, Let Flow

I would love to live
Like a river flows,
Carried by the surprise
Of its own unfolding.
—John O'Donohue

The ultimate spaciousness to me is the feeling of gliding through life without friction or resistance—quite literally.

It's the feeling you get when you're floating down a river, watching the ocean waves come and go, meditating by a fountain, sitting by a crackling fire, or listening to a gurgling mountain spring.

Adopting a daily practice of slowing down unleashes all kinds of magic powers, which lead to greater ease and flow and morph into new habits that expand your sense of spacious well-being.

Or, to put it more simply, slow, flow, grow, glow . . . in that order, cycling in a continuous, easeful loop.

For one student, a minute of slowing down "flips the switch" from effort to ease:

> I need it [slowing down] . . . especially after a busy stretch when I am pushing myself too hard to stop and listen. Flip the switch—so easy, yet so out of reach sometimes, as if getting on a plane and flying to another world. Yet I'm learning it can be done instantaneously, and by choice. The one minute makes the idea of slowing down more bearable. And then, when I choose the minute of stillness, the entire flow of my day changes.

You never know what surprises might emerge or unfold when you're traveling in the slow lane. It could be an unexpected gift of birdsong or church bells in the distance that transport you even further into heaven. It could be a call from someone delivering really good news. It could be the feeling you get when all the green lights seem to sync up just for you.

And here's the thing: you don't have to leave the comfort of your chair to get better at this slowing down thing and receive its soothing benefits. A song or video could be just the thing to soften resistance, quiet the mind, and calm the nervous system.

Practice

In what ways can you cultivate more ease, flow, and stillness in your life?

The practice this week is to live this question. Pose it out loud, wait for the answers to emerge, and then act on them every day to the degree that you are able. If the answer is to spend more time by the ocean and you live miles from the nearest beach, for example, choose another body of water that would serve this purpose, even if it's your bathtub. Or search YouTube for videos that might give you a yummy experience of ease, flow, and stillness by the sea.

If your mind finds all kinds of excuses to avoid slowing down, your practice this week is to sit with and feel the resistance as it arises without judgment, every day, until you experience greater flow.

Journal Revealings

⬦ Ways that I can cultivate more ease, flow, and stillness in my life are . . .

◇ Stuckness feels like . . .

◇ Flow feels like . . .

WEEK 5

Soften Resistance

The mystic has seen that the meaning of being alive is just to be alive. . . . It is so plain and so obvious and so simple. And yet, everybody rushes around in a great panic as if it were necessary to achieve something beyond themselves.

—Alan Watts

If you've wondered why anyone would want to dial it down when life might be more exciting in the fast lane, consider this simple fact: It's because you're missing the show!

Eat a meal too fast, and it's no secret that you don't connect as well with its nourishing effects, the flavors, the people who prepared it, the people you're eating with. Rush through a "tedious" daily task like folding laundry or putting dishes away, and you miss out on the calming, meditative effects that a simple housekeeping practice offers.

Go on a wild binge of clearing out a closet and you miss out on the opportunity to identify garments that truly make your heart sing or to lighten your load from the inside out and connect with the reasons you're holding on in the first place.

In a very counterintuitive way, slowing down can actually lead to greater productivity. As one student shares here:

> I've noticed an unexpected ease and patience with clearing things and thoughts. Inch by inch we are making space in our basement. I'm typically an impatient person, rushing from one project to the next. I'm slowing down. What a relief! In the past I would have given myself a weekend to do the impossible. Or just not do it. All-or-nothing mentality. Now I'm just giving what I choose to give. And it is still getting done. I'm witnessing a more spacious life.

As Lao Tzu so beautifully reminds us: "Nature does not hurry, yet everything is accomplished." Or as I like to say, we go slow to go fast.

It takes time to soften resistances that are deeply embedded in our physical, mental, and emotional attachments. We need time to rewire a brain that goes into fight-or-flight, time to grow new habits that feel really good and create lasting change. On the other side of our resistance is a treasure waiting for each of us. All we need is to slow down enough and loosen our grip to claim its blessings.

Sounds good, doesn't it? Except that there's one more (very big) detail.

Slowing down by itself isn't going to get us very far in clearing if we don't include the one thing that makes it all work:

awareness. Taking the time to observe resisting patterns as they arise—without judging them—is the secret to clearing them.

How do we know that we're bumping up against some old, crusty resistances? We feel them. For example:

◇ Your breathing . . . Is it shallow? Are you holding it in?

◇ Your mouth . . . Is it dry? Are you clenching your teeth? Are you suddenly very thirsty?

◇ Your hands . . . Are they hot, cold, clammy, grippy, tingling?

◇ Your belly area . . . Do you have a knot in your stomach? Are you nauseous?

◇ Your legs and feet . . . Are they wobbly? Do they ache? Do you feel ungrounded?

◇ Your thoughts . . . Are they racing?

◇ Your emotions . . . Do you feel irritable? Frustrated? Overwhelmed? Want to fight? Want to flee?

If you can bring compassionate awareness to these stressful energies disguised as "aches and pains," they will release their grip on you and give you your power back, once and for all.

Awareness is your superpower here. The sooner you can make friends with it, the sooner you will be free of anything that holds you back.

Practice

What do you notice when you slow down? What happens when you allow your resisting patterns to simply bubble up without judging them?

Your practice this week is an opportunity to consciously slow down and shine light on the spaciousness that lies on the other side of your resistance. Choose a simple task that you can repeat every day (preferably at the same time) that might bring up some squirmy resistance. Do something that is mildly challenging, something that's maybe not your most favorite task but is not so daunting that you'll lose heart and give up. It could be a home-tending task like doing the dishes, preparing a nice meal, or tackling that gardening project you've been putting off. It could be addressing one small task a day from your long list of to-dos: like sewing the missing button back on your favorite sweater (requiring you to dig deep in the closet to find the needle and thread), replacing the light bulb on your front porch, or taking your car in for an oil change. Whatever you choose, slow it down and give it all of your attention.

And just to be clear, this practice is not about gaining mastery over a task or even making progress on it. It is simply an opportunity to notice what happens to resisting patterns when you bring your awareness to them. The task is not the end point. It is your pathway, your vehicle to spaciousness.

Journal Revealings

◇ I've chosen this task or process to dial down every day this week . . .

◇ When I slow down and observe the squirmy resistances that come up, this happens . . .

◇ What I'm discovering on the other side of my resistance to slowing down . . .

WEEK 6

Take Your Time

Things take the time they take. Don't worry.
—Mary Oliver

For all of us, time can seem to stretch and contract in incredible ways. A difficult conversation seems to happen in slow motion, while a weeklong vacation whizzes by in an instant. Yet the clock ticks in a steady rhythm. How can this be?

There is a scientific reason, no doubt, which I couldn't begin to explain. What interests me more is what stress does to warp our concept of time and promote scarcity thinking and how conscious slowing down can counter this force. This is a topic I can speak about with a certain degree of confidence now after a fascinating discovery I made a few years ago.

I was doing something that I had never done before: I was making a series of videos to help launch and promote my second book. For someone who is more comfortable teaching in rooms with real live humans than in front of a camera, I was way out of my comfort zone (read: terrified).

It took weeks to figure out what I wanted to say and more weeks to write the scripts, distill the material even more, and rehearse. I found a free teleprompter I could use on my laptop and spent another week doing endless practice runs, tweaking the speed levels—not too slow, not too fast—so I could look effortless in front of my audience. I hired two videographers to come shoot at my house.

On the day of filming, I was ready. Laptop: check. Teleprompter set at the perfect speed: check. Husband in the room cheering me on: check.

I was good to go.

But when the camera started rolling, suddenly it felt like the lines in the teleprompter were flying by in a blur. I was so breathless I could barely keep up. I was talking a mile a minute, way too fast for my comfort.

Take two. Same thing.

The truth is that nothing had changed—except I had. I was a nervous wreck.

It took moving on to videos two and three (before going back to the first one) to finally find my groove, to finally feel like the teachings I had so carefully distilled could be delivered with the love and passion with which they were created.

ou haven't figured it out by now, it was stress rearing its
le head, bending time, and making me feel crunched
for it. We don't need science to explain the myriad ways stress
messes with our minds, including how we process the passing
of time. We can *feel* it. In the end, it pretty much boils down
to this: decrease stress and increase calm, and you will find that
time is much more elastic, grooving at your speed.

So, take your time. There's a lot more where it came from.

Practice

How do you relate to time? What does stress do to your concept
of time? What happens when you take your time, consciously
and deliberately?

Use this week to play with time. Notice when and how it races
by, and what's going on in your life when it feels like it's slowing
down in a good way. Mix it up. See what happens to your sense
of time when you do the same thing over and over again: same
routine, same tasks, same habits. Notice what happens when you
change things up, perhaps by trying different foods, adopting a
new skill, or visiting a place you've never been to before.

Journal Revealings

◇ When I feel stressed, I notice that time . . .

◇ When I take my time consciously and deliberately,
I notice . . .

- When I do the same things over and over again, I notice that time . . .

- When I consciously disrupt my routine, I notice that time . . .

WEEK 7

Unplug

Almost everything will work again if you unplug it for a few minutes, including you.
—Anne Lamott

One day when we were vacationing on Cape Cod I came across a young woman on a bridge wearing a red dress. The sun was setting. The light was extraordinary. I zoomed in with my iPhone and clicked.

Then I noticed that the young woman didn't seem to be enjoying the same light that I was. She seemed lost instead in the light beaming out of her smartphone. There was beauty everywhere, and I felt a pang of longing for her to turn away from her device and enjoy the show that I was seeing all around her.

Have you ever considered how much wonder and beauty we might be missing out on because of the time we spend glued to our electronic devices? What would happen if you took a mini-break from checking your emails, texts, messages, and social media threads for the rest of the week?

Gulp.

I'm not asking you to actually do this, mind you—just suggesting that you consider the idea . . . and feel the gulp.

And if it moves you, you can finish reading this lesson and unplug for a while. Who knows? You may just find yourself experiencing a few spacious benefits, like what Waylon Lewis, founder of Elephant Journal, shares here:

> When we break away from the busyness and superficial activity of technology-drunk daily life . . . time slows, the world becomes more vivid, and we fall in love with our life, again.

Seems like a pretty good trade-off to me.

Practice

What does being plugged in feel like? What are some pleasant surprises or things of beauty that catch your eye when you unplug?

Before you begin your exploration, let me just clarify that this week's invitations to unplug are *not* intended to disconnect you from your lifelines or livelihood. They are simply an opportunity to bring greater awareness to any unconscious habits that disconnect you from living your life more fully now, in the present moment.

The practice is twofold.

1. **Record**: For the first half of the week, keep a log of how much time you spend online (that is not work-related)—checking Instagram, Pinterest, Facebook, or newsfeeds, shopping online, or whatever your thing is. Write down what you tune in to, the times you tune in, and the length of time you spend on each. You could try the same exercise with what you watch on TV, listen to on the radio, etc.—basically, anything you do that feels noisy and repetitive.

2. **Reduce and release**: For the second half of the week, reduce the time you spend on these activities by half (or as much as you can handle) and use that time to do something else instead. Notice how hard or easy it is to unplug. Notice the cravings—the sticky attachments—and let them come and go without doing anything to fix, manage, or change them. Notice signs of irritation and pushback (i.e., feeling annoyed, deprived, put upon, pressured by "unreasonable" demands, etc.) and what happens when you breathe into the prickly resistance.

Journal Revealings

◇ The amount of time I spend plugged in, online, and watching screens is . . .

◇ Types of resistance that arise in me when I unplug . . .

◇ What I notice when I bring my full awareness to my resistances and breathe into them . . .

◇ Pleasant surprises that I'm beginning to notice when I unplug . . .

WEEK 8

Be the Witness

Rather than being your thoughts and emotions, be the awareness behind them.
—Eckhart Tolle

One of the benefits of slowing down is that it gives us space to practice that one thing we can all use more of: spacious detachment, which I would define simply as a way of being bigger than our fears and tears through the conscious act of observing them.

Being a witness in this sense is a deep form of attention that we give to an experience without getting plugged into it, like watching a movie as it is playing out without getting lost in the story line, drama, or character's flaws and personalities.

While it might sound cold and heartless, being a detached observer is far from that. It is quite the opposite, in fact. As a witnessing presence you allow yourself to feel everything that arises deeply and compassionately. The only difference is that you are not taking the feelings personally.

This begs the question: How do we observe without attachment and feel deeply at the same time?

It's a bit like riding a bicycle and not falling down. In the beginning it requires focus and mindfulness. Later it becomes automatic: you simply *are* both unplugged and compassionate at the same time, able to handle the bumps that come your way without even thinking about it.

It takes practice to take in a bigger view than the narrow focus on what is causing you pain. It takes practice to grow the spacious muscle you need to embrace emotional charge without getting plugged in, or unhinged, by it.

There's a nice visualization that can help you detach. It was suggested by a reader in response to a blog post I wrote called "Clearing with Non-Identification: Be the Observer." For our purposes here, I'm calling this jewel of a tool the panning-out process:

> The one thing I find that works to unplug from a situation that has gotten me riled up is to back off in my mind. Like a movie camera that pans out, taking in the entire surrounding scene instead of focusing up close on the detail, I pan my mind back and out until I see the whole picture. It works amazingly well to focus off the intense drama, anger, or pain at the center. Pan out. See the background? See the light behind the angry face?

See the window behind the person in the foreground? See the flowers blooming and blowing in the breeze outside the window? Take a deep breath. Feel better. Dis-identify. This is not about me. This is just another scene in a long, long movie. Don't make it so important. Put it in perspective. Relax. By the end of the movie, this scene will hardly even be remembered.

If panning out like a movie camera doesn't help you detach from the drama of the day, you could reach for something that comes built in: your breath. Close your eyes and focus on your breathing for one minute. As you breathe, use phrases that start with the words "This is . . ." to practice detachment. For example, instead of saying, "I'm late!" you could say, "This is a delay." You can detach from whatever annoys you (and plugs you in) by breathing and changing how you frame it.

Practice

Is there something that's bothering you right now that could use some spacious witnessing? What happens when you observe the feelings without getting caught up in the emotional weather, the story, or the drama that triggered it in the first place?

Use this week to play with your powers of compassionate observation on any issues that are weighing you down. Identify an issue that is bothering you, and adopt it as your daily practice exploration for the week. Use the journal prompts to help get you started.

Journal Revealings

◇ Something that's bothering me is . . .

◇ What happens when I zoom out with my imaginary camera lens or consciously breathe into the emotion . . .

◇ What happens when I slow down first and then observe . . .

WEEK 9

Wander and Wonder

Look around you at all things unnoticed. Look up at the distances contained in the sky, and the mystery underneath your feet. Bathe in beauty's soothing balm.
—Mary Oliver

Every day on my walk I am struck by the old-world beauty of a meadow with a single bench that seems to be saying, "Join me, take a load off, stay awhile."

The fact that it's just a few yards away from the historic home of transcendentalist writer Ralph Waldo Emerson is no small detail. My experience of this place is so timeless that sometimes I feel like I'm going to bump into the man himself, inviting me into his world: "Hey, pull up a bench, let's enjoy this beautiful place together."

Is there a place you like to go that transports you in a similar way, a place that gives you a deep sense of timeless ease and peace? Is there somewhere you can go to simply be with your inquiries and allow the answers to find you? Take, for example, some of these heartfelt wonderings by my students:

I have been thinking a lot about stuck energy lately. Now that I have ended a relationship that has been bogging me down for years, I find that I have boundless energy to clear other things out of my life. When he calls or texts, wanting to maintain a 'friendship,' I find that I get stuck again, for days, feeling off-kilter and wondering why I am so tired . . . I ask myself why it is so hard to say the final 'No.' I get stuck in pleasing mode, even though I realize that it is detrimental to my health and well-being. Who am I pleasing? Perhaps my unpleasable parent who is long gone?

Today something really happened to me, and I was able to feel much freer to speak and able to organize my thoughts better. Maybe I am letting go of some of the attachment to outcomes and surrendering to what is. It was not a mechanical thing. It was as if my thoughts and actions were just able to flow. Wondering if this is a result of the slow drips over the past weeks and months.

Has reading these stories awakened your curiosity, or raised any questions? (It doesn't have to be anything big or mystical. Just the fact that you're being stirred is enough.)

If the idea of taking some time to wander and wonder doesn't move you, here's a thought to ruminate on: What if the creative process is a two-way street? What if an inspired idea has a mind of its own and has been trying to get you to pay attention to it?

Just a little something to a-muse you. ;-)

Practice

Is there something (big or small) that you've been noodling on that could use some quiet space to sort itself out?

Use this week to sit in quiet contemplation every day, and let the wonderings flow—in your head and in your journal. Take yourself to your favorite bench in the park or the woods behind your house. Do it even if it appears that there is nothing to contemplate. Notice how ideas come and go and if, or how, they try to get your attention.

Journal Revealings

◇ A place that I love to go to is . . .

◇ Wonderings, curiosities, or stirrings that are awakening in me . . .

◇ Ideas and answers that are finding me . . .

WEEK 10

Drip, Drip, Drip

The journey of a thousand miles begins with one step.
—Lao Tzu

Is there something you've been dreaming about? Do you have a recent passion or a lifelong desire to dive into or accomplish something? Or is there even just a habit you'd like to change, adopt, or grow?

For years I have wanted to devote more time to one of my first, all-time loves: photography. When I found out that a teacher whom I've admired for some time was going to be in town teaching one of her programs, I jumped at the opportunity to study with her.

Weeell, sort of.

I didn't dive in. I "dripped" in. I put my toe into the idea and swished it around.

I hemmed and I hawed.

I waded and waited.

I expanded and I contracted.

I talked myself into it. I talked myself out of it.

And only after all that back-and-forth was I able to cut through the noise and remember to adopt my slow drip process—which, in this case, looked something like this:

1. Check my calendar and make sure I was free to take the class.

2. Consider whether I have enough financial spaciousness to fund this extracurricular activity.

3. Watch my mind play games with my heart and try to derail my efforts: *It's too expensive . . . It's too far away . . . What if it's too hard? . . . What if I don't like it?*

4. Breathe into the fears, objections, and resistance, allowing them to come and go without judgment until the stuck energy starts to lighten and lift. *(This step is key.)*

5. Sign up for the class.

6. Repeat Step 4 every time that grasping, chattering, fearful part of the mind (also known as monkey mind) starts ranting again (*Yikes, I'm doing this! Can I get my money back? The class is next week!*).

Drip. Drip. Drip . . .

Now maybe my example is too big of a challenge for you to chew on right now. Maybe all you want is to reduce your caffeine intake, for example.

If you break it down into small, doable, conscious steps, this is what your slow drip might look like:

1. **Intend:** Set the intention that you will drink one less sip of coffee a day.

2. **Reduce:** Pour a bit less coffee or tea into your cup than you're used to.

3. **Observe**: Watch your mind play games with you.

4. **Feel**: Sip slowly, and breathe into and feel any resistance (crankiness, impatience, frustration) that arises.

5. **Circle back**: Repeat Steps 1–4 tomorrow, and every day for a week, and notice what happens.

6. **Review**: Notice the shifts, not only in your caffeine consumption, but in how this practice morphs into clearing other "consumptions" as well.

You can adapt these steps to address any challenge, problem area, or habit that you would like to change. In Step 2, for example, you can "reduce" anything that best matches the task or situation. You can reduce in terms of quantity, area of focus, or time spent.

In the end, whether it is a nail-biting problem you are trying to break, losing excess weight, or learning to set clear boundaries with others, it's important to remember that this practice is ultimately *not* about the issue that is holding you back. Nor is it about the desired outcome. It's about how you *relate* to it. It is the space between the issue and the outcome where the real goodies are, where the real clearing happens.

And a good way to become a master at this is . . . you got it . . . *to slow down.*

Or as I like to say, small steps equal big changes.

As we close this section on slowing down—the first "S" to spaciousness—I can't think of a better way to celebrate than to steep in mystical harmonies hiding in plain sight that can only be heard when sounds are slowed way down. To hear what I'm talking about, go online and google "crickets slowed down."

The symphony produced by these creatures—the harmony of them all connecting on the same wavelength—is truly spellbinding. It feels like the curtain is being pulled back for a brief moment and we're being given an exclusive peek into the sublime mysteries of the Universe.

Whether the sounds are real, or a manipulation of sounds manufactured in a studio as some people claim, perhaps you can let your heart take over. Can you allow yourself to steep in wonder, in the idea of mystical expression?

Can you imagine what *you* sound like when you slow down?

If you needed any more reason to dial it down, let these sounds remind you that you too came to shine your light brightly.

Practice

What has slowing down over the past ten weeks meant for you? What treasures are you uncovering when you ease up on the gas?

The practice this week is twofold.

1. **Engage**: Bring awareness to something you have been dreaming about and wanting to accomplish—recently or for your whole life. What are the fears that are keeping you from doing it? What are some small steps you can take each day this week to

soften the resistance and move you closer to making your dream happen?

2. **Reflect**: Take some time to go back through your journal and highlight the lessons and practices that really worked for you. (Come back to these down the road when you need reminding.)

Journal Revealings

◇ One thing I've wanted to accomplish more than anything is . . .

◇ The fears that I'm aware of that have gotten in my way in pursuing my dream . . .

◇ Simple steps that I can take to soften resistance are . . .

◇ What slowing down over the past weeks has meant to me . . .

◇ Ways that I will continue to cultivate this practice of slowing down . . .

◇ Treasures that I'm beginning to uncover by dialing it down . . .

PART 2

SIMPLIFYING

Our life is frittered away by detail. . .
Simplicity, simplicity, simplicity!
—Henry David Thoreau

Welcome to simplifying—our second step to spaciousness. Like with slowing down, it too has magical powers—especially when you adopt it as a daily practice and infuse it with awareness.

If the prospect of simplifying seems uninspired or boring, or too small a gesture to address the chaos that lives in your head, home, or heart, consider this scientific fact: When you reduce a task into smaller, doable steps, and repeat the task, you effectively bypass the fight-or-flight triggers in the brain and rewire it. Over time, this reduces internal clutter, noise, and overwhelm—*for good.*

Taking a simpler, baby-step approach to life ultimately makes it possible for us to accomplish a *whole lot more.*

And a whole lot more means a richer, more inspired, and more spacious life.

Does this sound good?

Part 2 will ease you into it.

WEEK 11

Simplify

simplify *(transitive verb)*
: to make simple or simpler: such as
a: to reduce to basic essentials
b: to diminish in scope or complexity: streamline
c: to make more intelligible: clarify
—Merriam-Webster Dictionary

So what does it mean to simplify as it relates to clearing our homes and lives?

It's pretty simple, really. As the word implies, simplifying can mean reducing physical excess. It can mean quieting the noise and mental chatter. It can mean allowing emotions to arise without getting lost in their story or drama by being compassionately aware.

The rub, of course, is that in order to become masters of simplicity, we need to enter the thicket where complexity lives and reigns: the noisy head and the unhealed heart.

And how do we navigate these messy spaces quietly and gently without getting lost or sucked in by them? We already have the tool. It is something we've been practicing for ten weeks already. It's called slowing down.

Yes, slowing down naturally leads to simplifying. And simplifying, in turn, helps promote slowing down. They work very nicely as a team. As you connect these two steps, you'll discover one of the quickest ways to get unstuck and create more flow in your life. It cuts right through the noise fast.

Here are a few examples of what simplifying might look like:

◊ When you don't know what to say, simplify. (Say less or nothing at all.)

◊ When you can't decide what to wear, simplify. (Choose a single color.)

◊ When nothing is going as planned, simplify. (Pick one feeling you'd like to have in the day, and release all expectations for how things should go.)

◊ When your heart is broken and you can't make sense of a major loss and disappointment, simplify. (What do you need in this moment? Comfort? Connection? Energy? How can you give yourself that thing in some small way?)

◊ When you're at your wit's end, an exhausted heap on the floor, having tried everything, been everything, and still it's not enough, simplify. (What is

the next smallest step toward your goal—a really
tiny step? Do that.)

And if you don't know how to simplify, just ask yourself:
What is one small way that I can simplify in this situation?

And wait for the answer.

All you need is one step as a first step.

Sometimes just asking the question is a way of simplifying.

For me right now, for example—moments after discovering
that an entire batch of laundry came out of the washer covered
in a million tiny pieces of Kleenex—simplifying means throwing the whole wad into the dryer as is, and sitting in my rocking
chair next to a sunny window.

Yes, that's what I'm doing as I write this: letting the sunshine
bathe me with heat and light. And I already feel better.

What goes through your head when you consider that your
life really could be a whole lot simpler, while still being rich and
enlivening at the same time?

Let's find out, shall we?

Practice

What is one thing in your life that could use some simplifying
right now? What would help you shift the energy fast?

Use your journal this week to brainstorm or free-associate
your way to simpler solutions to problems you are facing using
the prompts below. It might also help to break your idea down
into the tiniest steps using the slow drip method that you practiced in Week 10.

Journal Revealings

◇ One thing in my life that could use some simplifying is . . .

◇ One thing I can do to move the energy to a solution could be . . .

◇ Using the slow drip method, it might go like this . . .

WEEK 12

Move Things
to Move You

*The art of dwelling happily in the present
moment is the practice most needed in our time.*
—Thich Nhat Hanh

One of the best teachers I know who can help us get really good at simplifying is not a person. It's a place. A place that is always there for us regardless of how we treat it: our home.

And when we slow down and bring compassionate awareness to our *tending* of this place, that's when some real magic starts to happen.

Take, for example, the simple task of moving things around. It could be rearranging the books in your bookcase, changing the position of your utensils, or placing your coat hangers facing out instead of in to begin identifying the clothes you don't wear from the ones you do. You can even take a line out of Marie Kondo's *The Life-Changing Magic of Tidying Up* and ask yourself, "Does this object spark joy?" It's a great way to give your possessions a new lease on life (and you too, by extension).

You never know where your practice might lead. It could give you the urge to purge or nudge you to look into some little dark corner of your life, as some students share here:

> I had been thinking that I really wasn't feeling any changes coming from [my small changes]. But then out of the blue I have this overwhelming need to get rid of this desk made from an old sewing machine that my father had restored.

> I changed ONE thing in my kitchen (moved the knives to a more useable spot), and next thing I knew I was emptying my spice cabinet, throwing out spices I have had forever, and reorganizing and making ROOM. That led me to another cabinet, and my husband even joined me for a bit (reaching high shelves and carrying heavy things), and in a few hours we'd rearranged the whole kitchen, cleaning as we went.

> Yesterday I did some more tidying up of my filing cabinet. But when I came to the fat folder of "marriage—

divorce," I quickly shut the drawer again. Today I feel curious about this. I wonder what is in the folder. Is it time to clear up some old issues with compassionate awareness?

When I first read the section in Kondo's book inviting us to take a joy pulse of our possessions, I immediately began scanning the room I was in: my living room. My eyes landed on the cluster of mirrors that had been hanging on the wall for nearly twenty years.

I could tell right away without even holding them that they no longer sparked joy. I put the book down and started taking the smaller ones out and moving the larger ones around. It didn't take long to feel a sense of sparkly possibility, more space, more breathing room.

After about twenty minutes of playing musical mirrors, I liked the feeling of having fewer objects on the wall. Same mirrors. Fewer of them. New placement.

That whole room now sparkles with joy!

That said, if I had adopted Kondo's discarding technique, as she suggests we do with anything that does not spark joy, it's possible that I would have thrown out all the mirrors and never known that they still could make my heart sing.

In my experience, even just one minute spent moving things around can tell us a lot—not just about our home spaces, but ourselves. It also does wonders to move energy that has been stuck for a while, which can create an opening that wasn't there before. It may not amount to much at first, but if you repeat the task every day, over time you effectively create more shifts and more openings that start to amount to something, something tangible you can feel and see.

Like more clarity. And inspiration. And light.

Practice

What happens to your energy level when you move things around? What happens to your energy level when you bring all of your awareness to a simple task?

This week, you'll get to find out by attending to a single drawer. Whether it's the utensils drawer, a sock drawer, the glove compartment of your car, or whatever calls your attention, the practice every day this week is to spend at least five minutes attending to it by following the steps below.

And again, just to be clear: the purpose of this practice is *not* about having a clear drawer. It is not about satisfying an itch to fix a problem area. It is not about seeing how much you can accomplish in five minutes.

This practice is simply an opportunity to lighten your load from the inside out: to clear *you* by using a drawer as the pathway and your teacher.

Observing the squirmy resistances that might arise (without judging them as bad), noticing how your body processes stuck energy (getting unstuck), and feeling subtle energetic shifts and openings when you move things around *is the work*.

That, in a nutshell, is clearing.

Attending Process

1. **Inquire**: Choose one drawer to work with and ask yourself before opening it: *Do I know what's in this drawer? Do I love and use what's in this drawer?* Notice your breathing as you say these questions out loud. Notice how you feel.

2. **Look inside**: After you've had a moment to tune in, open the drawer and look around. Do nothing else but notice your thoughts and feelings. Notice your breathing again. Has it changed?

3. **Rearrange**: When you feel complete, move things around—slowly. Rearrange the objects, or move a pile from one spot to another, while observing your thoughts. Notice any physical sensations. For example, is your mouth suddenly dry? Is your breathing shallow? These can be signs of you processing stuck energy.

4. **Discard or relocate** (optional): If it moves you to discard or relocate some of the contents, do so with awareness. Again, notice your breathing. Has it changed?

5. **Close**: When you feel complete, close the drawer, and close your eyes. Do you notice any shift in energy in your self?

6. **Repeat**: Follow Steps 1–5 with the same drawer, or a new one, each day for a week.

Journal Revealings

⋄ Taking a moment to reflect on the contents of a closed drawer makes me feel . . .

⋄ Moving things around (rearranging, discarding, relocating) with awareness makes me feel . . .

⋄ Some of the ways that energy appears to be shifting and lifting in my life just by tending to a single drawer each day are . . .

WEEK 13

Clear for Beauty

Have nothing in your houses that you do not know to be useful, or believe to be beautiful.
—William Morris

One of my colleagues shared a photo on Facebook of a drawer that she had just organized. With each object tucked neatly in its little home, it was thing of beauty. I loved that she had consciously chosen things that were colorful and beautiful to look at. I know that if it were my drawer, my heart would go pitter-patter every time I opened it!

When you think about it, our efforts to organize our possessions or clear them are mostly about improving functionality and lightening our load. Beauty is usually an afterthought.

What if each of us spent a week clearing an area of our home with the sole purpose of making it not only functional, but beautiful as well? Like art. What would be the effect of adopting beauty as an operating principle in every clearing task you take on?

There's a useful tool I presented in my first book, *Your Spacious Self,* that can help with this. I call it the "stay, go, throw, don't know" pile method. It is a simple way of sorting and clearing your possessions on the fly while helping to clarify what stays, what goes, what matters, what doesn't. It's also useful as a memory aid whenever you feel overwhelmed or distracted.

Here's how it works: when clearing an area of your home, organize your stuff into these four piles:

Stay: Things you need, use, or love that stay put.

Go: Things you need, use, or love that have not been put away or have migrated from their regular "home" (e.g., reading glasses, TV remote, car keys).

Throw: Things you're ready to discard or recycle.

Don't know: Things that are a dilemma. This is hopefully your smallest pile. The idea here is to give yourself a little time (no longer than a week) to think about where the item(s) should ultimately go.

While this process was originally designed to help you move through your stuff quickly and efficiently, like a card dealer at a casino, I might suggest a different, slower, approach: notice what happens when you attend to your piles and spaces more mindfully and reverently and beautifully.

Clearing mindfully for simplicity as well as for beauty can be very calming and harmonizing and fun, especially when we follow our heart.

Think of it as heart work, not hard work.

Practice

What happens when you slow down and clear for beauty as well as efficiency? What is the most beautiful, functional thing in your home and why?

The practice this week is to clear for beauty by following the steps below. Choose a drawer that you worked with last week or a new space that is calling your attention. If it helps in your process, I invite you to take a "before photo" to measure your progress later and remind you how far you've come.

Clearing for Beauty

1. **Keep it simple**: Set aside five to fifteen uninterrupted minutes and choose a drawer or space to work with; keep your focus on small and doable.

2. **Group**: Remove all contents and group them into four piles: Stay, Go, Throw, Don't Know.

3. **Beautify**: Consciously return the "Stay" objects to this space—one at a time—in the most beautiful way possible: group by color, texture, and utility. Move things around. Tweak until your heart registers a "click." Consider having some empty space in there, too, to invite possibility.

4. **Tune in**: Notice how the new space makes you feel every time you connect with it.

5. **Observe**: Notice if this simple practice leads to other areas of effortless clearing and beautifying.

Journal Revealings

◇ A small area of my home that could use some beautifying . . .

◇ What it feels like to sort my things more slowly and mindfully . . .

◇ What it feels like to open a drawer or closet that looks like a thing of beauty or work of art . . .

◇ What I consider beautiful in my home . . .

◇ Ways I can cultivate more beauty in my home . . .

WEEK 14

Make the Bed

If you want to change the world,
start off by making your bed.
—US Navy Admiral William H. McRaven

I love making the bed in the morning. I love smoothing the bunched-up sheets at the foot of the bed, shaking and restoring the comforter, fluffing up the pillows, placing them back, tucking the bedspread over them, and finally, like a maestro putting the last flourishing touch on her art, laying the silk accent pillow in the middle. *Voilà!* I step back and take it in. I love looking at it every time I pass by the bedroom.

It takes, *what,* five minutes to practice this daily ritual and meditation? It is pure pleasure, and it sets me up for the rest of the day.

It seems I'm not the only one who has a thing for making the bed. (Retired) US Navy Admiral William H. McRaven has a thing for it, too. In his now famous commencement address at the University of Texas, this former Navy Seal cuts right to the chase. In less than two minutes he makes a very compelling case for how making one's bed can change the world. While there is no mention of extra-comfy refinements that can make a bed feel nurturing and inviting, his message has real merit. You can find a link to my favorite clip of his speech in the back of this book.

Whether you're a fan of this daily ritual or not, here's what I can tell you: there's making the bed and there's *making the bed.* The first is the way most people approach it: in a rush, on autopilot, or not at all. The other, lesser-known way, is slower, more mindful, with love.

Adding mindfulness to something you do—or could do—every day gives you a bounty of clearing benefits, too. It can give you an inside peek into your resisting patterns. It can show you where you feel stuck in your body. It can reveal the torrent of unconscious commentary running unchecked through your mind, as one participant of my online courses shares here:

> While simply making the bed yesterday, I noticed all the negative self-talk prior to starting, such as, *Oh my God, there is so much to do today and I still have to make the bed!* Then I realized my stomach was tight and my body was tense.
>
> While making the bed, I fought perfectionist tendencies, also glancing at the time that was running out, already future-tripping about all that I have to tackle next on my long to-do list.
>
> As I fluffed the pillows, thoughts of people wronging me would pop up, as well as things I wish I would've said or done. Regrets, getting pissed off at myself and others, worrying about the future—all this popped up in less than five minutes. This was also mental clutter I needed to clear. So I practiced breathing as I smoothed

the sheets, noticing the silky texture and warm colors. That was when my body relaxed. Because for once, I was in the present!

You see, without naming what we're thinking and feeling—as it is happening—we cannot begin to clear it. Five minutes of mindful bed tending not only smooths out the bunched-up sheets, but it gives us a perfect opportunity to smooth out all kinds of other bunched-up, resisting behaviors that keep us stuck as well.

In my view, this is how making the bed can be life-changing.

Game-changing.

And yes, even world-changing.

Practice

What can you learn about and clear in yourself by mindfully making the bed? In what ways does this one simple task ripple out to change the way you relate to other tasks you've been avoiding or resisting?

The practice this week is to make your bed slowly every day. Put as much mindfulness and love into it as you can. Notice what goes through your mind and any sensations in the body. Notice the impulse to rush and "get it over with." Notice what it feels like later to come back to a bed made with love. Use the witnessing tools from Week 8 to soften negative self-talk and resistance.

Journal Revealings

◇ What it feels like to make my bed every day with complete awareness . . .

◇ What I notice when I *consciously* make the bed . . .

◇ I love making my bed (and getting into it later at night) because . . .

◇ Some enhancements I could add to make my bed look and feel better . . .

◇ Some of the ways that this practice ripples out to change the energy in my home . . .

WEEK 15

Sweep in Simplicity

We are sweeping—a kind of delicate dance which results in this dirt being outside now with the other dirt—moved on. I want to be here with this moving on, moment to moment, sweeping.
—Gunilla Norris

If you've followed my teachings, you probably know that I'm a big fan of sweeping. And if you're rolling your eyes, going, *Here she goes again with the lesson on sweeping*, let me ask you: When was the last time you picked up a broom? Or swept a floor with your whole heart and awareness?

Exactly. We forget. If not the sweeping part, we forget the awareness part.

When it comes to experiencing quick relief fast, there is nothing better than your old trusty friend, that thing on a stick squirreled away in your kitchen closet: your broom.

Add one minute of awareness to this task—or any housekeeping task, for that matter—and you've raised your game to a quantum level.

The simple act of sweeping with awareness isn't just great for moving cobwebs out of your house; it has a magic way of releasing the cobwebs between your ears as well.

It's an excellent tool to use when you're noodling on something, can't see your way to a solution, or feel just plain stuck. As a daily practice, it works equally well to invoke a fresh start, anchor an intention, cultivate mindfulness, and calm the noisy mind and nervous system.

While the task itself has you thinking you're working on something "productive," the truth is that it has a wonderful way of working *on you*—charming you—into a deep place of contentment, while it quiets the part of the mind that feels it needs to be in control.

Reach for a broom today, and let it all go.

Who knows, you might even experience a moment of quiet spaciousness that was not there before.

Practice

Is there a question that you've been noodling on lately? Is there an issue that has made you feel stuck or overwhelmed? Are you resisting something?

The practice this week is to sweep in simplicity by sweeping one area of your home every day—with all of the awareness you can muster—to gain greater clarity, reduce the stress you feel, and soften resistances you might still be lugging around.

Journal Revealings

◇ One thing I've been noodling on is . . .

◇ What I notice when I bring my full attention to sweeping . . .

◇ Resistances I have that I would love to soften and release . . .

WEEK 16

Fold In the Magic

If you fold your clothes in the formal spark of joy, you can actually make the joy last longer.
—Marie Kondo

I am often asked by readers and students if I've read Marie Kondo's *The Life-Changing Magic of Tidying Up*. After all, we have a lot in common. We both were organizational geeks as children. We both believe in imbuing our possessions with love and expressing gratitude for their service when we let them go. We both see home tending as a pathway to personal transformation.

I've not only read her book, I've put some of her tidying suggestions to the test in my own home. Many of Kondo's methods dovetail nicely with the simple principles I teach and write about here.

Folding is one example. Besides mindful sweeping, folding clothes and putting them away are some of my most favorite ways to nurture simplicity and ease. I love this for what it does to calm the nervous system and quiet the mind.

Reading Kondo's book, I learned there is an art to it as well. Her method sounded beautifully Zen, so I wanted to try it. She suggests a technique that allows for garments to be stored upright in a drawer to create more space, making it easier to find them later, and freeing clothing from getting piled upon, which creates more wear and tear and wrinkles.

So, one muggy afternoon, I tried it with all of my clothes: socks, tops, T-shirts, scarves, underwear, nightgowns, swimwear. One drawer after another, I eagerly went to work, replacing my usual "fold over once" habit with the more precise, multistep KonMari system of folding.

And fold-by-baby-step-fold, I could not believe my eyes. I was amazed—giddy, in fact—to discover how much empty space I was creating, to see that the same quantity of clothes could take up less than half the space!

From bureau drawers I eagerly moved to the shelves in the closet, pulling out more things and throwing them into piles on the bed. Sweaters, sweatshirts, sweatpants, cargo pants—all the bulkier things—underwent the same makeover with the same astonishing transformations.

But at some point folding fatigue began to set in. I watched my giddiness turn into a heap of exhaustion right there with everything else on the bed. My body hurt from top to bottom. My brain was in a fog. Clearly, I had taken on more than I could handle in this first round.

While this exercise ultimately proved to be a game changer, I'd be lying if I said that folding the KonMari way was a walk in the park. It was not. Here's why:

⋄ Folding takes time.

⋄ Folding in a mindful way takes even more time and focus when you're new at it.

⋄ Moving piles of clothes around moves stuck energy.

⋄ Moving stuck energy doesn't always feel very good when it's been around for a while.

If you're too excited to slow down (as I was), too excited to pay attention to telltale signs of moving the layers of stuck energy trapped inside your drawers and closets, adopting a binge approach can take its toll.

The good news is that there is a way to fold (organize, clear) that is not so taxing. It requires making some adjustments that involve the first two S's: slowing down and simplifying. Here are some tips on folding in the Spacious Way:

1. **Simplify**: Work one drawer at a time and notice your energy level before, during, and after. Set a timer for fifteen or twenty minutes, if you have to, so you don't blow out your circuits.

2. **Be mindful**: Handle each garment, as Kondo suggests, with more appreciation for its function in your life (rather than focusing on getting it right). Remind yourself that this is a practice, not a race.

3. **Take it in**: Admire the beauty of seeing your clothes neatly stacked in their vertical bundles. Celebrate the ease of knowing where everything is and the joys of having more space.

4. **Intend**: If there is something you wish to attract in your life, invite this newfound space to act as a symbol and a magnet for it to come into being.

5. **Have fun**: If you're having fun, keep going. If it feels hard, stop, and give yourself a self-care break.

6. **Repeat daily**: Follow Steps 1–5 until the task is complete.

In the end, you do not need to fold and put away everything perfectly *just so* to receive the spacious benefit that the practice offers. In fact, the idea of perfection might well be counterproductive. If the KonMari way of folding feels too overwhelming, rigid, or time-consuming, I would suggest you dial it back and adopt the gentler, "slow drip" approach you learned in Week 10. Fold your garments in a way that feels right to you and put them away with love.

If you're willing to ease into the process and give yourself time to integrate the changes, I think you'll agree that folding in the Spacious Way is worth it.

But don't take my word for it. Try it this week.

Practice

What could use some conscious folding? How does the Kon-Mari method stack up, as it were, with the usual ways you tend to your clothes?

This week's practice is twofold (pun intended).

1. **Watch**: Google a video or two of Marie Kondo folding. You can start with the link in the back of this book under Resources. Notice her hands, how they move and how she uses them to connect with the garments. Notice the love that she imbues into each task. Notice how her demeanor makes you feel. (Spoiler alert: it could be very calming.)

2. **Fold in**: Identify a small area of clothes that could use some folding and follow the steps above for folding in the Spacious Way. Start slow, with a garment or two, and work your way up to drawers and closets as energy permits. Notice physical sensations, resisting patterns, and shifts in energy and record them in your journal.

Journal Revealings

◇ The clothes that could use some folding today . . .

◇ What I notice before, during, and after doing this task . . .

◇ What it feels like to fold the KonMari way and how it contrasts with my usual way of folding . . .

◇ Spacious modifications I can use to make it work better for me . . .

WEEK 17

Tame the Piles, Quiet the Overwhelm

Life is simple. It's what we believe
about life that complicates it.
—Byron Katie

When I read the section on clearing paper and paperwork in Marie Kondo's *The Life-Changing Magic of Tidying Up*, I must confess that my eyes started to glaze over. I felt overwhelmed and tired. I couldn't focus. Her suggestions for how to manage paper clutter were a blur. The only method that made sense to me was "discard everything," and that was too much for me to process at that moment in time.

This is not her fault. Paper is one of the biggest challenges facing most of us. When I surveyed over ten thousand students, readers, and SpaceClear followers, I was struck by how many of them said paper was one of their biggest clutter challenges.

Even I, the veteran space clearing practitioner and teacher with decades of experience, still have way too much paper.

I pushed past my initial blur (aka resistance) and kept reading. When I landed on the part where she talks about credit card statements, warranties, and appliance manuals, I perked right up! *This* I could handle. And being told that I didn't have to keep any of it was a complete revelation and a relief.

You mean I can ditch the two years of credit card statements that I meticulously save for who knows what?

You mean I can toss the appliance warranties—those scary-looking yellowed papers—that I never filled out which have long since expired?

You mean I can throw out the manuals with intricate illustrations on how to install my appliances?

Radical!

So out they went: credit card receipts, warranties, and yellowed manuals for appliances (some of which we no longer owned)—direct into the recycling bin.

It took me less than fifteen minutes.

That was day one.

On day two, I pulled out my beloved recipe box that I've had for over forty years, the one with the homemade tabs I made with that embossing gizmo that was popular in the seventies. I threw out half the contents: over 110 recipes, which I've lovingly kept all these years just in case I'm inspired to make brown bread, Orange Julius, or spice sachets.

Not gonna happen. Not. Ever. In. This. Lifetime.

Reducing the Overwhelm

If paper—or something else—is a huge challenge for you, if it paralyzes you or makes you go into cold sweats just thinking about it, that would be a big indicator to dial it down and simplify. In my years of clearing I can tell you with absolute certainty that it's nearly impossible to make progress when we're in a heightened state of alert or if we're overwhelmed.

You can blame the brain.

Overwhelm happens when an ancient part of our brain, called the amygdala, has been activated and triggers a cascade of stress hormones through the system. You've probably heard of it: it's called the fight-or-flight response.

It's like our built-in secret service agent that springs into action the moment it senses danger. It's a great thing to have when you're being attacked by a wild beast or your toddler is reaching for the kitchen knife. It's not so useful when you're confronted by insane piles of clothes or having to deal with a difficult boss or family member.

The rub is that once the stress response has been triggered, there really is no automatic off switch. The mechanism works more like a motion sensor—you know, like those lights that turn on when someone walks by.

When fight-or-flight switches on, it *stays on,* as long as it continues to be activated through attachments, painful memories, fearful thoughts, or some other strong emotional charge that we've been carrying.

The cycle of overwhelm that is wreaking havoc on the nervous system, making us procrastinate, or making us want to bury ourselves in more stuff, or food, or TV, isn't going to stop until *we* stop—stop the recycling of fear or pain or emotional charge, most of which is unconscious.

I know, *bummer,* right? Can you see now why we might need to simplify?

Moving the needle out of the red zone of overwhelm takes work. The good news is that with consistency, practice, and awareness, we can rewire the stress response and break the cycle of overwhelm *for good!*

For us to reduce overwhelm, three things need to happen:

1. We need to slow down—just like we've been practicing already.

2. We need to focus on tasks that do not set off alarm
   bells in the brain.

3. We need to be consistent with our efforts, which,
   in this case, means *daily*. Not just on weekends, not
   just when we feel like it or can squeeze it in.

Let's say, for example, that your desk is driving you insane.
It is constantly getting slimed with papers, bills, loose change,
gum wrappers, etc. Instead of doing what most impulses dictate,
which is either to attack the mess or avoid it altogether, what you
want is to adopt a gentler approach that does not send you con-
tinuously into a lockdown of frustration, despair, or exhaustion.

Here's how to tame the piles and the noise behind them:

1. **Rule of One**: To cultivate greater focus, you can
   adopt the "rule of one"—one piece of paper, one
   pile, one area, one minute, one day, etc. My recipe
   box is a good example: I chose the contents of that
   one box to work with in one sitting—not the folders in my filing cabinet, which also need clearing;
   not the letters that still sit in a box in my closet.

2. **Reduce and Repeat**: To cultivate consistency
   and tiptoe around the amygdala, you can try the
   gentle "reduce and repeat" approach to clearing
   ("R&R" for short). What this means is that you
   reduce a task (area of focus and/or time spent on
   a task) until it no longer elicits the stress response

and you repeat it, every day, until the job is complete, even if all you can handle is a single paper clip or moving one pile from one corner of the desk to another . . . little by little . . . one step at a time . . . one breath at a time . . . with all the awareness you can muster. Keep repeating it until you begin to see that gleamy empty space on your desk and in yourself.

I can already see the eye rolls and hear the groans and protests: *But . . . but . . . I have so much stuff. . . . At this rate it will take me a lifetime to clear it . . .*

Here's what I have to say about that: That's the overwhelm talking and not the real you.

If my baby-step method is making you cringe because of how lame or ineffectual it seems, let me tell you what is really going on under the radar when you adopt a simple, conscious, slow drip approach to clearing: it creates new neural pathways in the brain, which grow new habits, that start to feel good . . . like, really good . . . and magically expand into more effortless tending of other areas of your home and life.

Whether you choose to work with your magazine or stamp collection, the condiments in your refrigerator, or your shoe stacks, the rule of one and the R&R approach work like a charm to ease the stress you hold and soften your resistance to it.

Plus, it makes it a lot easier to address the bigger elephants in the room, like your paper clutter.

One day you'll find yourself in front of your Mount Everest of paper with more energy and aliveness than you ever imagined. You'll be flipping right through it, watching it fly out of cabinets and shelves into your recycling bin, without as much as a flinch, all because of a simple, daily tending of other things that may not even be related!

Practice

Do you have paper (or something else), or does it have you?

Use this week to tame some piles and quiet the noise by adopting the rule of one (one piece, one pile, one area, one sitting, one minute) and the R&R approach to clearing.

Remember, if you feel even a tad bit overwhelmed, you've gone too far. Keep "reducing and repeating" your tasks until they no longer elicit the stress response. If paper or whatever you're working with is too much to handle right now, choose an area of clutter that you can address. Bottom line: slow down and keep it simple.

Journal Revealings

◇ Piles that I'm ready to pull out and work with . . .

◇ What it feels like when I get overwhelmed . . .

◇ Tasks that I can reduce and repeat . . .

◇ When I set clear boundaries for myself and work with just one thing (pile, area, minute), I notice . . .

Lighten Your Digital Load

*When things aren't adding up
in your life, start subtracting.*
—Unknown

If I had a clearing theme personally this year, it would be the year of the pixel.

More specifically, the year to clear my massive collection of unloved and unseen photos (over 36,000, to be exact) that have been taking up space on various generations of laptops since digital photography was invented.

Yes, I know. It's insane.

It would have been far easier to just delete the whole lot of them with one flourishing swipe and start fresh. (Believe me, I wanted to do that a million times.)

As a longtime lover of pictures since I started taking them at the age of ten, however, the task of deleting with abandon was not an option. My heart needed to go through every last, single, boring, fuzzy, duplicate photo and clear it mindfully until the job was complete.

Inside those digital albums are countless memories that I wanted to be able to reach for and enjoy—like the cute pictures of my daughter boogie boarding each summer on Cape Cod;

the once-in-a-lifetime visits to the home of the US ambassador to Italy and his wife in Rome; and the rich assortment of classes, students, and book signings that played a big part of my life over the past twenty years.

I can't lie and say that it took me a week to do this one task. Dipping into my digital past took me six months.

Here's why it was worth it and why you might want to consider taking this on as a long-term project:

It's all energy: From an energetic standpoint, digital clutter is no different than physical clutter. Just because it isn't tripping you in the hallway doesn't make it less worthy of your attention and efforts to clear it.

It's lightening: Releasing digital clutter—be it photos, emails, files, contacts, bookmarks, etc.—releases stuck energy. It lightens your load and opens the channels for something new to come through.

It's enlightening: The process of clearing gives you a terrific opportunity to bring compassionate awareness to the thoughts and feelings that can come up—like the noise you hear when you look at old photos: *Ugh, my hair looked awful back then ... Who is that guy ... ? When is this task ever going to end ... ?!*

It's a practice in simplifying: As with any practice that you repeat regularly, it gets easier over time.

It's habit-forming: Consciously releasing your digital clutter in small, doable batches has a magical way of easing you into clearing the bigger physical, mental, emotional clutter that might be stressing you out.

It's fun: Little by little, you'll begin to see that you are creating a new system that is easier to access and can change your life. With photos, for example, you've not only created a vibrant record of your life that you can share and reach for whenever you want, but you've put in motion a whole new organizing principle that can change everything.

What is one area of digital excess and noise that could use some turning down this week? If you don't have a clue, I invite you to dust off some of your favorite practices in slowing down and simplifying to help you gain some clarity so that you can take the first step.

Remember, when you dial down a task, you have an opportunity to reduce overall stress, overwhelm, and any resisting patterns that might be keeping you stuck and unable to move forward.

Drip, drip, drip . . .

That's how we roll.

Practice

Do you have photos on your devices that you haven't looked at in a long while (read: years)? Are your emails, files, folders, contacts, bookmarks, or apps out of control? Do you even know what you have squirreled away on your devices?

Use this week to begin lightening your digital load by following the process below. Because this project will likely take longer than a week to complete, I recommend you bookmark this page to come back to in subsequent weeks.

If pixels are not picking at you, reach for something that is, such as photo albums, books, or collectibles, and use the same steps below to clear them. The process is the same no matter what you choose to work with.

Lightening the Load Process

1. **Take inventory**: Go through your devices and make a list of everything that needs clearing or deleting.

2. **Choose one**: Select *one item* from your list to focus on this week and apply the rule of one (see Week 17): one folder, one album, one batch, one hour. Be discerning, and only work with what you think you can handle. Add more "ones" later in the week as time and energy permit.

3. **Set a goal**: Set an intention for this one task this week. With my photos, for example, I set a goal to delete all the boring, fuzzy, or duplicate images that no longer added value or made my heart sing. Refresh and recommit to your goal each week.

4. **Go slow**: Start clearing/deleting. Give yourself as much time, space, and slack as you need. Remember, this is not a race.

5. **Reduce and repeat**: If you start to feel overwhelmed, dial it back and adopt the R&R approach (see Week 17): reduce the task even more and repeat until it no longer triggers your fight-or-flight response. For example, instead of one folder, choose one file; instead of one album, choose one row of photos; instead of one hour, choose one half hour.

6. **Stop and feel**: If you begin to grow exhausted, bored, despairing, or even nauseated by the sheer enormity of the task, stop, name, and experience the discomfort, and do something else until you feel better. Be the witness: observe the thoughts without attaching any drama to them (see Week 8).

7. **Get support**: If it's too much to handle, consider who might be able to help you and call them. In my case, I called Apple Support a number of times for guidance on how to upload my entire library to the cloud and sync all my photos.

Journal Revealings

◇ The digital load (or other load) that could use some conscious and gentle pruning is . . .

◇ When I prioritize, it looks more like this . . .

◇ What I notice when I set clear goals and boundaries
for a project like this . . .

◇ What it feels like to lighten my load (and changes I'm
noticing in my life as a result) . . .

WEEK 19

Care for the Soul

*Tending the things around us and becoming sensitive to
the importance of home, daily schedule, and maybe even
the clothes we wear, are ways of caring for the soul.*
—Thomas Moore

The other day I saw an ad for a folding machine. No joke. It's a
big, clunky thing into which you insert your shirts, towels, and
whatever else you've got, and *voilà!* Out they come, all nicely
folded. It made me think of TV ads from the 1950s, rolling out
all kinds of gadgets promising to save us time.

While it's a fun, innovative, and compelling idea, I can't see
how a device like this simplifies your life. I'm not sure it saves you
any time, frankly. You still have to feed the thing a certain way.

And then you have to find a big space to store it . . .

And maintain it . . .

And miss out on the nourishing effects of folding clothes the old-fashioned way and putting them away with love.

Why would you want to miss out on that?

Why would we want to miss out on the beauty that reveals itself when we move things around with awareness? Or the balance that is restored when we slow down and honor our things—like our bed, our broom, our clothes? Or the ease and quiet that comes from tending to our piles and digital loads one baby step at a time?

If these simple tasks give us ways to care for our soul, why would we want to miss out on that?

Hopefully by now you are beginning to see that our practices in simplifying are not about having a perfectly made bed or neatly folded clothes, beautiful drawers or sparkly floors. It's not about sorting and tidying, beautifying and quieting.

It's about what caring for our spaces does to soften and nourish and transform us. It's about the heart and presence we bring to a task, no matter what it might be, and the spaciousness that naturally arises from that.

That's what this is about.

Practice

In what ways has simplifying and caring for your home these past few weeks nurtured you? What tasks or objects have helped you feel more spacious? What tasks or objects no longer serve and support your highest and best good?

The practice this week is twofold. Choose different days to focus on each exercise.

1. **Reflect and appreciate**: Walk around your home and notice the love that you've slowly and consciously "dripped" into it over the past few weeks. Open drawers or cupboards that you have beautified with loving care and be lifted by them. Thank your broom for its service. Give your bed a smoothing pat of appreciation for its support over the years. Revisit your clothes, tucked neatly in their drawers or shelves, and make any additional adjustments or tweaks. Take a moment to breathe a sense of calm and gratitude into your space.

2. **Identify and clear**: Walk around your home and identify any objects that you once loved, used, or "needed" but no longer serve you or feed your soul. Thank them for their service and let them go with love.

And P.S., if either of these practices brings up feelings of inadequacy, self-doubt, or shame ("I could have done more. . . . Who am I kidding? . . . My home is still such a disaster. . . ."), use your time this week to dial back and attend to the "piles of judgment" with as much awareness and compassion as you can. This too is caring for the soul.

Journal Revealings

◇ What it feels like to contemplate my home and things with presence and appreciation for their function and beauty in my life . . .

◇ Ways that tending my home has nourished my soul . . .

◇ Tasks and spaces to which I can focus more love and attention . . .

◇ What I'm ready to let go of that no longer nurtures or supports me . . .

WEEK 20

Round the Bend

Things are not getting worse,
they are getting uncovered.
—Adrienne Maree Brown

Imagine a spiral staircase. It could be made of wood, or stone, or it might even be suspended in space. As we wrap up this section on simplifying, the spiral staircase is a symbol that can help us understand the work we've been doing over the past twenty weeks.

It reminds us that, like with all journeys, once we've set our intentions in motion and acted on them, we don't necessarily get to see the big picture all at once or know what we'll encounter around the bend. It's more of a process, an unfolding.

In the case of this yearlong process, for example, we might not fully know how slowing down and simplifying is making a difference; we might not fully see the kind of dent our daily baby-step practices are making to soften resistance and release attachment. We might have glimmers, but no real evidence as of yet.

We can only keep going . . . up, it seems . . . and in circles, it seems . . . though we don't know for sure.

And when we do, there comes a day when we realize that our efforts are having a magical effect. We'll "come around" and revisit a painful memory, an old habit, a stuck pattern, and discover that it eases and clears more quickly. It doesn't push our buttons as much. We have more energy and bandwidth and spaciousness to deal with it. There's more space. There's more light.

Yes, we discover that there is more light up here.

And we keep on going . . .

And every time we circle back around, we discover a new insight, a broader perspective, and a bigger heart to embrace a situation we couldn't deal with before.

And now it's getting exciting. We are not the same person we were when we started the climb. We are fitter, and happier, and more buoyant. We can handle almost anything that comes our way. We can see much farther.

We realize that progress is not linear.

And all we want to do is to keep going.

Practice

In what ways does the spiral staircase symbolize your journey so far this year? How have your small steps in slowing down and simplifying led to bigger changes? What new insights or heights of awareness have you gained?

As we complete our exploration of the second "S"—simplifying—the practice this week is twofold:

1. **Reflect**: Take some time in your journal to consider some of the ways you've grown and changed since you started "moving on up" twenty weeks ago. Reflect on small steps taken, insights gained, and your ability to handle challenges you couldn't imagine dealing with before. Even the tiniest shifts matter.

2. **Celebrate**: Honor your progress by going back through your journal and highlighting your successes, joys, or moments when the light seemed to shine more brightly for you. Use the exercise to remind yourself how far you've come—and how far you're going!

Journal Revealings

◇ New habits that I've adopted in slowing down and simplifying . . .

◇ Ways that things have shifted for me since I started this book . . .

◇ New awarenesses that I've had since starting this book . . .

PART 3

SENSING

The universe is full of magic things patiently
waiting for our wits to grow sharper.
—Eden Phillpotts

Life without the ability to feel is like a room without oxygen. It is time to turn up the light even more and dust off six tools that are massively important in our work with clearing: our senses.

Without our five primary senses of smell, taste, touch, hearing, and seeing, and our sixth sense of inner knowing, we cannot connect with our heart and the divine intelligence that comes through it.

Without the ability to feel, we have no way of knowing where we are stuck and where we are open, what sparks joy and what doesn't. Without our senses, we cannot sniff out a problem, see our way to a more creative solution, or feel to heal.

Because of our culture's emphasis on the intellect—on knowledge that can be seen and proven—we have become woefully desensitized. We are cut off from these remarkable gifts we came in with, our source of deep and infinite wisdom. And like a muscle that doesn't get used, our senses lose their strength and power if we don't nurture and apply them.

We can reverse the trend. We can channel more light, experience more wonder, and expand our range of what is possible by just simply *coming to our senses.*

Part 3 shows us how to play.

WEEK 21

Tune In and Tune Up

Still—in a way—nobody sees a flower—really—it is so small—we haven't the time—and to see takes time like to have a friend takes time.
—Georgia O'Keeffe

There's a flower that caught my eye at sunset the other day. The afternoon light was incredible, and there it was, doing its glorious thing of simply *being.*

I ran for my iPhone, zoomed in, and clicked.

Later, after I'd uploaded the image, I saw that it wasn't just a single flower anymore. Hiding in plain sight was a crinkled vine, shaped like an ampersand, and the dark leaves mixed in with the light ones—sibling buds at different stages of growth. All of it together, with the flower petals against the backdrop of the late afternoon sky, took my breath away.

Who doesn't love being stunned awake by beauty when you least expect it? The camera helps—and the willingness to slow down and detach from outcomes. There's a lot of magic out there just waiting for us to sense it. And, as Georgia O'Keeffe already reminds us, "to see takes time."

What do you notice right now that you hadn't noticed before? If you look more closely, what is it saying? What does it reveal about you?

It could be an object that you tune in to in all its glorious detail, or it could be one thing that leads to another and another, as one online course participant describes here:

> The light shining on the east wall leads me to where it's coming from—to the window of the door that shows me the sun about to set on this first day of the new year. I am drawn to go for a walk as the sun sinks below a horizon, turning a subtle salmon color . . . I welcome this new rhythm, this new pace, this new realm.

As we begin our exploration of "sensing"—the third stage in our journey together—let go of all preconceived ideas of what something should be, and enjoy the ride.

Be open. Be curious. Take your time. Allow whatever is wanting to reveal itself to you to do so. Adopt the Zen Buddhist attitude of *shoshin*, or "beginner's mind"—that is, bringing the openness and curiosity of an absolute beginner to any task and every moment.

Over the next ten weeks you will have an opportunity to experience the ease, beauty, and magic that comes from tuning in to (and tuning up) your six senses: seeing, smelling, tasting, touching, listening, and intuiting. You'll discover that the real show is standing right in front of you.

Practice

What is the first thing that catches your eye when you look up from this book? What do you see that you hadn't noticed before? What happens when you take your time to take it in? What does this say about you?

Use this week to practice *shoshin*: study your immediate surroundings from a place of beginner's mind. When you reach for your favorite coffee cup in the morning, for example, imagine that you've never seen one before. What do you love about it? How was it designed to be used? Is it practical? What's it feel like to the touch? Pay close attention to one thing for at least one minute every day, and record your impressions.

Journal Revealings

◇ What's catching my eye when I look up from my book right now . . .

- ◇ What happens when I slow down and take in my surroundings in this way . . .

- ◇ What it feels like to take my time taking in my world . . .

WEEK 22

Drink the Day

Set wide the window. Let me drink the day.
—Edith Wharton

One of the things I've enjoyed so much about having a camera by my side is that it helps connect me more deeply with more beauty. I love how it helps me slow down, focus my attention, and tune in to whatever shows up—in present time.

In photography, what I would call spaciousness could be called having "a good eye." And like with spaciousness, it is not some special gift bestowed only on artists. To the degree that we are clear, present, unattached, and open, we all have the ability to see the beauty and wonder that abounds. As photographer and teacher Elizabeth Watt describes in her blog,

> The *Good Eye* is a muscle we can build like any other. The fact that we have the camera now always in our pocket

is an advantage if used rightly—to tune in rather than tune out—as a practice it is incredibly enlivening.

And what does the "good" part of Good Eye mean, exactly? She explains:

Good here means that our mind is uncluttered by pre-occupation, relaxed and open. It's more about a letting go—of thinking, of preconceived notions, of labeling what we see. It's about *seeing clearly* without filters and biases . . . It's an internal, intuitive, fearless kind of seeing. It's a form of self-forgetting; it feels like flow. Photography approached in this way borders on spiritual practice, and images created in this space are the ones that resonate most with the viewer.

Whether it's summer flowers growing in the neighborhood, flickers of dark and light dancing through the kitchen window, a curtain blowing in the breeze just so, a random human doing something quirky, or a surprising pop of color when you least expect it, there is always something nudging its way into our field of perception, working its magic, quieting the mind, enlivening the senses, lifting the spirit.

Like a radio, all we have to do is tune in and receive it.

Practice

What happens when you take your camera out into your world and "drink the day"? What do you see when you tune in instead of tune out? What is your "good eye" practice revealing to you about you?

The practice this week is twofold:

1. **Tune in**: Once a day, photograph at least one or two things that capture your heart. Take an extra second or two to compose your shot before clicking the shutter. Try shooting from different angles, or zoom in for details. Notice the light, where it's coming from, and how it enlivens the scene you are drawn to. See if this simple daily photo exercise helps you slow down even more, become more present, and get clearer. If you don't have a camera, take pen and paper and sketch what you see.

2. **Expand**: If it moves you (and you have the capability), make a short video of something that captures your heart.

Journal Revealings

⬦ What I'm noticing when I drink the day with my camera . . .

⬦ What is beautiful about what I'm seeing . . .

◇ What my "good eye" practice is teaching me about myself . . .

WEEK 23

Look Around

All you need to do is be aware of your
thoughts and emotions—as they happen.
This is not really a "doing," but an alert "seeing."
—Eckhart Tolle

If you were to take one minute to look around your home, what things would you notice that spark the most joy? What does this quick scan say about you?

Today, my list of joy-makers might look something like this (in no particular order):

◇ The twinkly lights that wrap around our screened-in porch. I call them my mood elevator on a string. I love that they come with a remote control and that with a simple flick of a button you can change the color and increase or decrease the brightness. Every night as it gets dark, *bling,* on they go to lighten our lives no matter what time of year it is.

◇ My mother's old Singer sewing machine. You can still see the words "I love you" that I secretly scratched into the base when I was about seven years old. Every time I pull out this ancient machine to sew a seam or mend a garment, I am awed by its beauty, its functionality (yes, it still works like a charm), and the love that it represents (my mother made all of my clothes when I was a child).

◇ The three decorative birds made out of various forms of quartz that our Brazilian housepainter surprise-gifted us. Every time I look at them, I am reminded of the marvelous world we live in and the extraordinary generosity of a man we hardly know hauling these heavy beauties in his suitcase just for us.

And what does it say about me and my personal style? It might say that I'm partial to things that are old, bold, colorful, purposeful, magical, things made with love, things that remind me of people I love, things placed just so that the light can shine through them or be easily picked up and touched.

Maybe you're feeling that there are no sparks out there to be seen (yet) . . .

Yes, sometimes this exercise can take you to places in your home and heart that aren't so pretty or comfortable. Sometimes you need to uncover what's blocking your view. Sometimes you need to name your pain and feel (clear) it before you can finally rest on what you truly love.

Whatever shows up . . . or doesn't . . . in the end, it's all good.

Practice

What in your home catches your eye, captures your heart, and raises your energy level? What do these sparks say about you?

The practice this week is threefold.

1. **Explore**: Use this week to explore both your home and the world outside to identify the things that bring you the most joy. Notice what gets in your way. Notice patterns. If it helps, photograph these things as you walk around to help you make connections to reflect upon later in your journal.

2. **Steep**: Spend some time leafing through your favorite magazines, or apps like Pinterest or Instagram, to steep in more beauty and joy.

3. **Expand** (optional): Create an "ideal image" poster or collage that reflects the things in your home and life that you love. Use it to raise your energetic vibration and attract more of these things into your life.

Journal Revealings

◇ If I were to summarize some of the things that make my heart sing the most, they would be . . .

◇ What these objects say about my personal style . . .

◇ What these objects say about me . . .

Inhale

Paradise is not a place; it is a state of consciousness.
—Sri Chinmoy

One of the biggest pathways to my heart is through my nostrils—literally. I have a highly developed sense of smell.

It comes in handy, too. As a professional space clearer, I can sniff out energetic disturbances in a home a mile away. While not always pleasant, it can be a useful tool for identifying invisible stress and clutter in a place.

Still, for all the unpleasant side effects that my schnoz can bring with it, there is a big upside as well. The ability to imbibe some of nature's sublimest aromas is one of the best things on earth, if you ask me. Plus, following my nose has led me to be able to follow my "knows" over the years and has never led me astray.

If we were to repeat the exercise from last week's lesson, but instead of objects choose our favorite aromas, here's what my "five scents list" might look like (in no particular order):

⋄ Clothes that have been hung outside to dry. Who doesn't love the fresh smell of clothes that have danced with the breezes and been kissed by the sun?

⋄ Fresh-baked bread. Right. Out. Of. The. Oven.

◇ Lavender essential oil. In a hot bath or on a pillow, it does wonders to soothe the soul.

◇ Garlic sizzling in olive oil. Works every time to get me out of my chair and hang my nose over our cast-iron skillet.

◇ "Double Delight," a red-and-yellow rose. This hybrid tea rose has won awards for its fragrance. No wonder I love it.

Now it's your turn. What smells get your attention? What aromas make you go weak in the knees or swoon with delight? What would it take for you to cultivate more of them in your life?

Practice

Take some time this week to stop and smell the roses, as it were. Tune in to the whole spectrum of beautiful smells from your world and record them in your journal. It could be the crisp notes of a cup of Earl Grey tea or the mysterious fragrance of an exotic flower. Notice the ways that having an enhanced sense of smell can assist you in other ways, like "sniffing out" a good opportunity or a scam.

Journal Revealings

◇ Some of the smells that I encountered today that I love . . .

- ◇ If I were to summarize the smells that I most adore, they would be . . .

- ◇ One thing I can do to have more of them in my life would be . . .

- ◇ What my "knows" is revealing these days . . .

WEEK 25

Savor

Pour milk in tea but do not stir. Watch milk clouds and tea swirl together at the gentle pace they prefer.
—Henry Ponder

While traveling in France last year, my husband and I treated ourselves to a tiny, very fancy tin of chocolates. It came with this not-so-tiny set of instructions:

Plunge Into the Art of Tasting: To taste a great chocolate, take the time to awaken your senses. Observe the color, listen to the characteristic "snap," appreciate the texture on your tongue and enjoy it. You must learn to distinguish the first, highly-volatile aromas, giving the chocolate its length. This is when you will perceive the warmer notes such as caramel and roasted nutty flavors.

With luscious-sounding instructions like these from Valrhona, maybe we don't need an actual box of chocolates to wake up our taste buds and make us swoon with delight (though I wouldn't say no if you handed me one right about now). It reminds me of the Netflix series *Chef's Table,* which I love to watch because of how evocative it is. For someone who doesn't cook, this is saying a lot.

Watching *Chef's Table* is a holy moment. It elevates the culinary experience to new heights—of beauty, art, sensuality, spiritual devotion, wonder—like I've never seen on television before. Watch any episode, and you get a deep dive celebration of . . .

◇ Passion and ritual

◇ Delicacies and mouthwatering ingredients being gathered, smelled, tasted, chopped, stirred, fried, melted, coaxed, whispered to, and loved into new forms

◇ Chefs telling their rich, messy, epic, and deeply moving personal stories

◇ Magical table settings—from rustic campfires to elegant Michelin-star-rated dining rooms—that are nourishing eye candy in themselves

◇ Drop-dead gorgeous locations and music

All of it together is a feast for the senses. For foodies and non-foodies alike, this show delivers, inspires, transports, and, most of all, feeds the soul.

If it sounds like I'm trying to sell you on something, I'm not. My gushing invitation, ultimately, is not about the show . . . nor the food . . . nor the rituals . . . nor how you set a table and enjoy a good meal.

In the end, it's about what cultivating these things opens up in *you* . . . and maybe even helping you to reach for that thing or passion that you've put off way too long, the thing that might give you your own taste of heaven.

Practice

What are some of the ways you can bring a little more heaven into your dining experience, your taste buds, and your life in general? What creative sparks awaken when you do?

The practice this week is twofold.

1. **Elevate**: Bring a higher level of beauty, awareness, and love to your dining experience at least once a day. Set the table, light a candle, buy some flowers, play soft music, use your best china—anything that transports you, raises your energy level, and enhances your sensory awareness.

2. **Savor**: Watch the official trailer for *Chef's Table* not just with your eyes, but with all of your senses. Which of your six senses is most awakened by the visuals and the music? If you are a Netflix subscriber, watch any episode in the series to stir you even more.

Journal Revealings

◇ Ways that I can bring a little more heaven into my dining experience . . .

◇ Ways that I can bring a little more heaven into my life in general . . .

◇ What doing these things awakens in me creatively . . .

WEEK 26

Touch Stones
(and Other Things)

Often the hands will solve a mystery that
the intellect has struggled with in vain.
—Carl Jung

There is a pile of roundish, colorful beach pebbles on the windowsill in our kitchen that I've collected over the years from our trips to Cape Cod. They're not just beautiful to look at, they're also wonderful to hold and touch and move around.

I love grouping them into circles, piles, straight lines; small ones on top of bigger ones; darker ones together; largest to smallest—whatever moves me in the moment. Sometimes I imagine they are little rivers or mountains. The combinations are endless, and so is the fun I have when playing with them for no purpose other than to see how much calmer I feel when I do.

I love running my hands across all kinds of smooth woods—chair arms, tabletops, spoons, our salad bowl made out of an old burl . . .

I love the feel of cool sheets in the summer and the nourishing softness of flannel in the winter. Have you noticed that organic cotton feels different than regular cotton?

What is something you love to feel with your hands? What is something that is instantly calming to the touch? Perhaps it's your favorite coffee cup or your dog's squishy toy or the silky freshness of cotton sateen bedsheets.

What does it feel like to be touched by a kindness—from a stranger, a friend, a family member—when you least expect it and need it most?

What are you noticing about your hands right at this moment? Are they hot, cold, tingly, clammy, tight, grippy, smooth, relaxed? What happens when you place your hand over your heart for a moment?

That's a good place to start.

Practice

What can your hands teach you about yourself?

Take some time every day this week to bring awareness to your hands and the wonders that come through them. Allow yourself to be drawn to different textures and materials and weights and notice what they feel like. Notice your impulse to touch someone who is hurting or receive someone's kindness when you are. Notice the vulnerabilities and fears that may arise at the thought of touching someone in a compassionate way or being touched.

Journal Revealings

◇ What I love to touch . . .

◇ What touches me . . .

◇ What I notice about my hands . . .

◇ When I place my hand on a body part that is contracted or in pain, I feel . . .

WEEK 27

Listen

The quieter you become, the more you can hear.
—Baba Ram Dass

Cicadas. Cars going down the street. Cars in the distance. More cicadas. Birdsong. Trucks backing up and beeping. Children laughing. A manhole cover clanking. More birdsong. Wind in the trees. Wind chimes. An unidentifiable beeping sound. A train going by. A train horn as it crosses the intersection. A train slowing down with a screech and stopping. More wind in the trees. A plane overhead. More wind . . .

That pretty much summarizes my one minute of active listening just now—in that order, sometimes in overlay—where I'm just allowing sounds to come and go like the wind in the trees.

What does your one minute of active listening sound like, and what is the quality of the sound? For example, are the sounds loud or quiet? Harsh or soft? Chaotic or coherent? Sharp or calming?

What happens when you turn down the noise in your life— the literal, and the metaphoric—and turn up what you would like to hear more of?

Practice

How noisy is your world? Your life? Which sounds do you find most soothing? Find out with this week's practice, which is twofold.

1. **Listen actively**: Take time every day to jot down your one minute of active listening in your journal. Rate these sounds—from chaotic to calm, harsh to soft, sharp to calming. Notice their quality and your tolerance levels, and bring as much spacious witnessing to these sounds as you can.

2. **Soothe your soul**: Make a video or audio recording of some beautiful natural sounds from your world. Have it handy and reach for it when you need a soothing lift or a heavenly pick-me-up.

Alternatively, you can reach for any number of beautiful soundscape selections available on websites and apps, like mynoise.net.

Journal Revealings

◇ My one minute of active listening sounds like . . .

◇ The quality of the sounds themselves feel . . .

◇ Some of the ways I can turn down the noise in my life (and what I notice when I do) . . .

WEEK 28

Needle and Feel

Clearing is like "needling" deep into the heart of all of our human fears and attachments in order to pierce and jiggle loose every last bit of squirmy, spasmy, unspacious stuff that's in there. It is our ability to be detached and available that invites disturbed energies in a space to magically reorganize and harmonize.
—Stephanie Bennett Vogt

As you may already know or have guessed, my work largely focuses on a system of clearing homes and hearts that has very little to do with the intellect. While my resources offer plenty of practical tips, tools, and how-tos to charm the rational part of our brain that is so eager to "fix" and "do something," the process of clearing itself is more sensory and intuitive by nature.

To the degree that you are not attached to a particular outcome, clearing the Spacious Way can deliver results at lightning speeds. And it is thanks to your six senses that all of this is possible.

The sensory muscles you've been developing over the past weeks—of seeing, smelling, tasting, touching, listening, and intuiting—are not only terrific pathways for experiencing more of that yummy light and beauty that abounds "out there." They are also an exceptional resource for processing and releasing more of the darkness and discord we all carry within.

And why might you want to rely more on your heart rather than your head when the results are so much harder to measure and quantify when you do?

One of the biggest reasons comes down to that coiled-up mess we all know so well: our emotions. The Spacious Way goes in deep to soften resisting patterns and dissolve the energetic charge they hold. Plus, it's more sustainable and lasting.

As yoga teacher Julie Peters illuminates so succinctly in *Spirituality & Health*:

> As much as we might try, our emotions are not controllable. They are not clean, separable entities we can put in boxes, label, and shelve. They are a tangled mess in our brains, bodies, and nervous systems. They can be triggered by an immediate event, or arise as an echo of

some experience we had years ago. We even have mirror neurons in our brains that help us pick up on the emotions of others—seeing someone cry makes us sad even if we have absolutely no idea why the person is crying. We can feel things that have nothing to do with us! There's nothing rational about emotions. They just are.

How do we untangle the mess? How do we know whose emotional "clutter" is whose? How do we identify and heal what is ours?

In a sense, none of that matters. Questions like these don't help us heal, because it's the mind trying to sort out what cannot be sorted out by way of the mind.

Emotions can only be observed and felt; witnessed and embraced—at the same time . . . in the present moment . . . without attachment.

In the end, the only way through to clearing whatever holds us back is to tune in to it with all of our senses.

Or, to put it more plainly: to come to our senses.

Spacious Clearing

While most of this book focuses on the "visibles"—that is, working with what we can physically smell, taste, touch, feel, and see—let's go deeper.

If it seems that it is just you, your physical self, doing the heavy lifting of slowing down, simplifying, and sensing, think again. There really is more to it than that. Or rather, I should say, there really is more to *you* than that. As Lynne McTaggart states in her book *The Field*: "Human beings are far more extraordinary than an assemblage of skin and bones."

In this week's practice, I will give you a taste of the extraordinary, spacious being that you are. In the guided meditation below I will connect you with your personal energy field. This is the expanded part of you that radiates out from the physical body like the growth rings of a tree. While invisible to most of us, it is in this huge, twenty-foot vibrating radius of our subtle anatomy where we store much of our "clutter" and where most of the deep, behind-the-scenes work of clearing is happening.

You don't need to take my word for it. It is not necessary to buy into the concept of an invisible energy field for this meditation to work its magic. Try the practice and decide for yourself. All it needs from you, when prompted, is your "attention on the tension" and a little "needling by feeling." The rest will take care of itself. With the witnessing and sensing practices you've been mastering over the past weeks, you have everything you need to take your clearing to a whole new, deeper level.

Practice

Is there something that is stressing you out or causing you emotional pain, unease, or discord? Lucky you, you get to clear it.

The practice this week is a spacious clearing process to help you "reduce, release, restore, and refresh": use it to reduce and release the emotional charge you hold around a stressful situation, restore balance, and refresh your entire being with cleansing, sparkly energy.

Read it as often as you need to get the hang of it. When you feel you have it, repeat the meditation with eyes closed and allow your internal guidance system to take over.

Spacious Clearing Process

Set aside at least fifteen minutes for this process. Find a quiet and comfortable place to sit, take a few swigs of water, and have your notebook and pen handy to complete the journal prompts that follow.

As with any kind of energy work, be gentle with yourself. If at any point you feel inordinately tired or uncomfortable, stop. Drink plenty of water, and practice extreme self-care. Give yourself time to grow the spacious muscle you need to do this powerful work.

1. **Center**: Take a moment to quiet the mind and check in with yourself by doing a full sensory body scan: Take a deep breath in and a slow emptying breath out and feel yourself growing relaxed and quiet and still . . . Notice your breathing: Is it shallow or full? How about your hands, are they hot or cold, prickly or tingly? Are you thirsty? Is there any tightness in your body? If so, where? . . . Notice what's going through your mind. Allow the thoughts to come and go, like the ocean's waves . . . There is nowhere you need to go right now and there is

nothing you need to do but observe, and feel, and breathe . . . Notice your energy level. Do you feel tired? Depleted? Excited? Curious? . . . Just keep breathing in and out as you become even more relaxed . . . and present . . . and still.

2. **Recall**: When you feel complete, tune in to something that has pushed your buttons recently, is stressing you out, or points to a strong emotional charge you might be holding. Whatever it is, go with your first impulse and give it all of your attention.

3. **Put the attention on the tension**: With all six of your senses (smell, taste, touch, seeing, hearing, inner knowing), notice what this issue feels like and where you feel it in your body. Notice your emotions. Give them all of your attention without trying to figure out what they mean or judging them as good or bad. Give yourself as much compassionate awareness, and space, as you can.

4. **Observe**: Notice if your witnessing of these sensations changes their intensity . . . and keep breathing.

5. **Gather**: When you feel ready, gather all of these sensations into a ball or a bundle of sticky (or stuck) energy. Add to it any loose bits of unhealed and unloved parts of yourself that are swirling around in your energy field (the invisible part of you)—all that discomfort, worry, fear, pain, shame,

guilt, regret, or not-knowing. Anything that weighs you down, does not serve and support you, nurture you, or feel good, feel free to add that too.

5. **Sense**: Notice if this expanding ball or bundle has a color or a sound. Notice if it has a taste or a smell. How heavy is it? What's it feel like? Keep gathering every last drib-drab of unpleasant, unfinished, gucky stuff until you feel complete.

6. **Imagine**: Now imagine a special golden needle that can release any level of stress that has been building up in your personal energy field—a needle that delivers the purest form of unconditional love, light, and healing presence there is.

7. **Insert**: When you feel ready, take a deep breath in and insert this needle into the ball of sticky or stuck energy. This needle knows exactly where to go and what to do. You don't need to do anything but focus your attention on the tension . . . and needle and feel.

8. **Needle and feel**: Keep leaning into the sensations with as much compassionate awareness and detachment as you can. Notice what happens when you simply wait and allow divine intelligence to take over. Give it time. Watch the process as it unfolds. Keep needling and feeling until something begins

to shift and reorganize into something quieter and more coherent.

9. **Witness without attachment**: Notice as this ball begins to lose its intensity, its charge, its grip. Watch as it gets smaller and smaller, like a balloon that is losing air . . . finally collapsing and dissolving . . . or floating away . . . or sloughing off . . . whatever feels right. Notice your breathing. Notice your energy level.

10. **Fill up**: Now bring your awareness to your heart and feel its compassionate, harmonizing, witnessing presence. Invite the divine unconditional love that emanates from your heart space to fill you up and restore you with cleansing, nourishing, healing light; to infuse every cell of your body—from the top of your head to the tip of your toes—until your entire physical self is brimming and shimmering with golden light.

11. **Beam out and smooth in**: When you feel complete, invite this divine love to radiate outward beyond the physical body: to act as a balm to smooth and integrate the clearing and to infuse your entire energy field until it too is vibrating and sparkling with cleansing, nourishing, luminous light.

12. **Surround**: Keep breathing in and out. Feel yourself expanding with each out breath, growing more

spacious and complete—beaming your awareness all the way to the edge of your personal energy field. Invite this divine light and love to surround you completely and act as a filter (a "discerning filter") to screen out that which no longer serves and supports your highest and best good. Ask that it help you maintain a clear, discerning, and sparkly personal boundary going forward.

13. **Tune in**: When you feel complete, take another nice, easy breath in and a slow, emptying breath out. Repeat the sensory body scan from Step 1 and check in with how you feel now. Notice if you feel the same or different than when you began this practice. Contemplate what it might feel like to live from this more expanded, heart-filled place.

14. **Journal**: Open your eyes. Bring your awareness back to yourself sitting in the room. When you feel ready, take a few good swigs of water, and use the prompts that follow to record your insights and deepen your experience of this process.

Journal Revealings

◇ A stress that could use some clearing . . .

◇ When I tune in with all of my senses, this stress feels . . .

◇ What happens when I put all of my attention on the tension and insert compassionate awareness into the area that is causing me pain . . .

◇ What I notice when I continue to needle and feel the emotional charge that this stress holds . . .

◇ What it feels like to be fully restored and refreshed (filled up, held, and surrounded) by the harmonizing frequencies of the heart . . .

◇ How I feel after this process . . . (and what I notice when I take this expanded feeling into my day and fold it into my life . . .)

WEEK 29

Shine Light

There's a crack in everything.
That's how the light gets in.
—Leonard Cohen

One spring day while walking past an old, run-down house in Mexico, I noticed light pouring through cracks in the door from the other side. There was nothing special about the moment—except there was. The door was so unassuming that I could easily have walked right past it. But I didn't.

There was something about the *light*—the way it pierced that door that took my breath away and brought me to my knees. Something about it made me feel like I was being touched by grace.

Unasked for, these spacious revealings have a way of showing up in all kinds of strange ways and places and usually appear when we least expect them.

What do your peepholes of light look like these days? In what ways do you feel that the light is shining more brightly for you?

It could be a shift in perception or an aha moment, like seeing something you hadn't noticed before. It could be a synchronicity or a repetitive encounter that gets your attention, like seeing 11:11 pop up on your digital clock, which in my case always feels like I'm getting a nudge from the beyond to pause and take a minute to feel what I'm feeling and express gratitude.

These peephole moments don't have to be some kind of mystical awakening or divine encounter, either. It could be the feeling of having more time to do things you love or the sense of deep calm you get from making the bed every day or putting laundry away. It can be the feeling of more bandwidth to deal with difficult situations or just plain old having more room to *breathe!*

It is these revealings of light—shifts in perception, surprise encounters, waking dreams, magic moments, symbols, connections with something larger than yourself—that I would like us to play with this week. In Week 21 we began our explorations of these, and now seems like a good time to circle back and see what new awarenesses are emerging.

Practice

How has your practice of tuning up your senses over the past weeks changed what you see and perceive? What is piercing its way into your consciousness? What is your world trying to tell you?

The practice this week is twofold.

1. **Connect**: Take some time every day this week to capture (photograph, sketch, collage, dance to, write a poem or melody about) a detail in your world that catches your eye, surprises you, or illuminates you in some way. Notice if, and how, your world is trying to get your attention and what it's trying to tell you. If you get no big revelations, don't worry. Use this exercise to practice beginner's mind and see what happens.

2. **Shine light**: Notice what your creative expressions have in common, if anything. Choose a few that reveal some themes or patterns, and write a caption for each one in your journal.

Journal Revealings

◇ What is catching my eye these days . . .

◇ Things that I am able to see and perceive more now than when I started sensing with awareness . . .

◇ How I see my world wanting to play with me (or not) . . .

◇ What my artistic representations have in common . . .

WEEK 30

Stir and Soar

I rest in the grace of the world, and am free.
—Wendell Berry

Cowbirds or starlings, I'm not sure what it was we witnessed in the high desert country of San Miguel de Allende, Mexico, at sunset last year—a ritual that happens every night in the winter months.

One word for this flock is a murmuration. But I call it happy hour for birds—masses of them, swooping in and out in exquisite harmonizing and mesmerizing patterns for about ten minutes before they settle down for the night. The divine intelligence that is at work keeping these creatures from crashing into each other is simply breathtaking.

I'd like to think that, at our very essence, all beings are connected and tuned in harmonically in the same way. If we stumble and bump into each other, it's because we've forgotten who we are. We've lost our way.

And that's what the five S's are there for: to help us remember, to help us gather all of our scattered parts and harmonize them so we can truly soar.

While our focus these past ten weeks has been on stirring things up—activating our senses of sight, smell, taste, touch, hearing, and inner knowing—as a way to tune in to and experience more of our innate spaciousness, there is an equally important "non-stirring" side to our clearing as well. This is where surrendering comes in—the fourth "S" in our journey—which is the ability to let go of attachment to desires and outcomes. As Thich Nhat Hanh writes in his book *Being Peace*, "For things to reveal themselves to us, we need to be ready to abandon our views about them."

As we get ready to transition into surrendering, the next stage to spaciousness, take a few moments this week to reflect on how sensing and surrendering might go hand in hand: how feeling your feelings fully and completely *and* letting go of attachment to them—at the same time—can take your clearing to a whole new game-changing level. Can you stir that into your awareness without stirring yourself into confusion and overwhelm?

To celebrate the completion of the third "S" and stir you into new heights, I invite you to watch one of the most extraordinary videos I've seen of a murmuration. If it has the same impact on you as it has on me, this two-minute experience will make you want to soar every time you watch it.

It's a Vimeo Staff Pick called "Murmuration," and you can find the link in the Resources section of this book. For full effect, watch it full screen and crank up the sound.

Practice

What happens when you allow yourself to be stirred?

The practice this week is threefold.

1. **Expand**: Reflect in your journal on the times in your life when you have felt completely expanded and filled with light and love. It could be good news that you received or a big surprise that you never expected. It could be a milestone or a completion of a long project that you've been working on for a long time, like a graduation, a finished manuscript, a marathon, or a marathon-like accomplishment. Tune in to those feelings again and fill yourself back up.

2. **Stir in**: As we ease our way into the fourth "S" of surrendering, reflect on the wonder questions of how you can feel deeply with all of your senses while at the same time being able to let go of attachment to those feelings. Consider how being able to do both at the same time does not diminish you, but rather expands and elevates you even more.

3. **Elevate**: Treat yourself to the two-minute video "Murmuration." Be sure to turn up the sound on your device and allow these mystical murmurations to lift and transport you.

Journal Revealings

◇ Some of the best, most expansive moments I've ever had in my life were . . .

◇ What it feels like to soar . . .

◇ What happens when I allow myself to feel the fullness of my being and let go of attachment to that fullness at the same time . . .

PART 4

SURRENDERING

Allowed doesn't mean agreed with.
It means seen, without rushing to oppose,
judge, deny, tell a story about.
—Jan Frazier

Surrendering is the fourth step in our journey together. If you are mystified by this one, you are not alone. The concept of surrender is one of the most difficult for us humans to get intellectually because it is not intellectual. Unlike the word implies, it is not about giving up.

Surrendering is more about stepping up (your game) by stepping back and allowing things to be as they are. It means being more of a compassionate observer of your experience as it plays out, instead of an attached observer.

To the degree that you are willing to be fully present and open your heart, the practice of surrendering will stretch you big time.

It will help you let go, lighten up, and transcend anything that holds you back. In our work with clearing, it's a game changer.

You won't be able to think your way through this one, I'm afraid. Surrendering is a way of being. And as Eckhart Tolle so wisely reminds us in his book *A New Earth*, "Being must be felt. It can't be thought."

How convenient that we've already had ten weeks of practice with sensing!

WEEK 31

Let Go and Let Flow

Don't try just be.
—Zap Mama

Before I introduce the subject of surrender with a story of my own, it might be helpful to do a little refresh of the five S's—slowing down, simplifying, sensing, surrendering, self-care—and what they do for us exactly.

As you may recall from Week 1, the five S's refer to the five keys, or practice steps, that we need to cultivate and sustain a spacious life. Integrating all five into a daily routine helps to soften resisting patterns, nurture real ease, and grow new habits that lead to lasting change.

There's a reason why these five S's are presented in this order—in stages. You see, you can't *simplify* without *slowing down*. Without a steady practice in *sensing*, you won't have the tools you'll need to step up your game with *surrender*. And without the nourishing effects of the first four S's that precede it, *self-care* has no ground on which to flourish.

The five S's build one upon another. They work together as a team.

Your dream team.

But for now . . . let's surrender.

To give you an example of what it means to surrender in real time, imagine me at home on a lazy Sunday morning when my husband decides to work on a project in the middle of the living room. I walk in with my coffee to see him all comfy and settled in a sea of his computer, cables, papers, empty teacups, and cushions.

It's no biggie, except that he has a home office. And it is Sunday. His taking over our common space on a Sunday morning, tapping away at his computer, royally pisses me off. It jangles my sense of order and proprietaryness (if that's even a word).

Right away I notice my resistance to it—that is, my desire and attachment to having the space be clear and quiet. I notice my breathing. I can feel a tightening in my chest, my mouth going dry, my teeth clenching.

Once I become aware of these sensations, I hang out with them for about thirty seconds. I focus my attention on the tension. I insert awareness into places that feel tight and contracted. I imagine a special golden needle delivering compassion directly where it is most needed—into where it hurts; into the chaos, stuckness, pain.

I notice that the situation is not personal and yet I've made it very personal. I'm still attached to being right—instead of happy.

I continue to needle and feel . . . needle and feel . . . and lean into things being as they are . . . until the resistance and the tightness begins to ease, and soften, and ultimately dissolve.

After about five minutes of personal space clearing in this way, I begin to feel more space: a calming of my nervous system, more breathing room, less attachment, a sense that I'm bigger than the problem that hooked me in.

I feel a wave of enormous gratitude and a remembering of what a blessing it is to have a life partner who is healthy, who loves me, who has work he's passionate about.

Yes, it can be a surprisingly quick turnaround. And in no small measure it's because of my willingness to hang out in this messy, uncomfortable in-between place, doing nothing but bringing as much compassionate awareness to a situation that I didn't ask for.

In other words, to stop "arguing with reality," as Byron Katie would say, and *soften into it*.

That said, accepting things as they are doesn't mean "settling." I can still voice my opinion. I can make my case for changing the situation. I can negotiate with my husband that he use a different space to do his office work.

What's different here is that I'll be doing so from a more spacious place, and guess what? He might be more available to listen to and receive what I'm saying from there.

Does that make sense?

That, in a nutshell, is what surrender means to me.

And what I haven't mentioned, but is implied and bears repeating, is that this is only *part* of what goes into success with surrendering. Your success with letting go is dramatically enhanced when you incorporate the other four S's of your team.

The good news is that you've been slowing down and simplifying and fine-tuning your senses for weeks now, and you've got some good tools under your belt. You are ready for this. You can do this!

Practice

What are you ready to soften into and surrender? What will you discover when you do?

Use this week to deepen your clearing practice from Week 28. Next time you get wigged-out by something or your buttons get pushed, give yourself five minutes to slow down, simplify, and tune in with all of your senses. Start with physical sensations and then the emotional ones: notice your breathing, your thirst, any tightness in your body, the tears and the fears, the sensations that you cannot describe. Once you've identified the pain and its location, imagine that you are inserting pure compassionate awareness to needle and ease some of the buildup of energetic pressure in these areas. Notice the shifts, if any, and follow up with some reflections in your journal.

(P.S. It might help to repeat the spacious clearing process from Week 28.)

Journal Revealings

◇ Something that is pushing my buttons today . . .

◇ Sensations that I'm noticing when I tune in to the discord . . .

◇ Shifts and ahas that I noticed after inserting compassionate awareness . . .

◇ What I'm ready to lean into more and surrender in my life . . .

WEEK 32

Make Space

I am a lover of what is, not because I'm a spiritual person,
but because it hurts when I argue with reality.
—Byron Katie

If there were a way to summarize in one sentence the fourth S—surrender—it would be in this beauty of a quote by master teacher Byron Katie. Who can argue with the logic? It *is* painful when we argue with reality, even if we're not aware that we're doing so.

But beyond avoiding pain, there is an even more compelling upside of surrender.

This upside came to me fully formed as an answer to a question I was having on one of my walks, a direct download from the Divine itself in the form of an acronym. My wonder question that day: What are the goodies that come from living a life of total surrender? If we can't think our way through it, how can we deeply understand it, embody it, and utilize it in our daily life?

Here is the transmission I received that day; what happens when you practice surrendering to what is:

Support: You expend less effort and connect with the ways the Universe has your back.

Play: You experience more joy by taking things less personally and yourself less seriously. This is also very *powerful*—another P.

Accepting and available: You learn to accept things in the moment just as they are, such as they are, which in turn helps you become more available to receive the blessings that want to come through you.

Care: Because you're more available you become less overwhelmed, which means more room to care for yourself and others.

Ease and expansion: You invite greater ease in all things, which in turn helps you expand your sense of self and the range of possibility.

Yes. SPACE.

What you get when you surrender is more space to live the life you were meant to live.

Wondering how to recognize the upside of surrender when it happens? If you could use some practical applications of this tool, here are some signs or markers to look for:

◇ **S**: Notice how you feel more supported by others when you don't jump to conclusions or make assumptions.

◇ **P**: Notice the powerful buoyancy you feel when you start to take things less personally and yourself less seriously. Notice how much more fun you have, and how much more attractive you are to others because of it.

◇ **A**: Notice the relief, and peace, you feel when you let go of attachment to an outcome. Notice the blessings the Universe showers on you because you are more available to recognize and receive them.

◇ **C**: Notice the decrease in overwhelm and the increase in ability and bandwidth to care for yourself and others.

◇ **E**: Notice the greater sense of ease and expansion you feel when you accept that some things are still a mystery and that you don't know what's going to happen next.

If you're not feeling too competent in the surrender department, no worries. Remember, this is not a race. Surrendering isn't something you "do" or "get."

It gets *you* and frees you.

Surrendering is a quality of spaciousness, a state of being that you cultivate and embody. Over the next few weeks you'll get ample opportunities to dip into that wellspring of surrender—beginning with this week's practice of recognizing it when it happens.

Practice

Got SPACE? Need more? How well are you doing with not taking things personally, attaching to outcomes, or arguing with reality? Use this week to find out and release some emotional clutter.

The practice this week is threefold.

1. **Review**: Reread the "signs to look for" above and notice the ones that got your attention. Which ones might be your growing edge? Focus more on those this week.

2. **Apply**: Using the signs to look for list as a guide, notice the specific ways you *experience* the benefits of surrendering in your life, and write them down in your journal. Even the smallest details matter. Keep the list close by to help you connect and remember.

3. **Needle and feel**: As you go about your day, notice the moments when you resist the natural flow of life and argue with it. What happens to your sense of spaciousness, instead, when you needle and feel these old contracting habits with compassionate awareness the moment you become aware of them? If you're game to go deeper, repeat this practice with a regret you've been harboring or a painful memory from your past: recall a difficult situation you could have handled with greater equanimity if you had had the tools. It could be a painful visit to your parents, for example, or a job interview that didn't go well, or a tense conversation with your ex-spouse. Practice needling and feeling the issue with as much awareness and compassion as you can until the memory holds no more emotional charge and remains simply that: a memory.

Please note: These practices are powerful when you give them your full attention. If at any point you feel overwhelmed by them or they bring up emotional weather that exceeds what you feel you can handle, ease up. Focus on something that holds less emotional charge and build up your spacious reserves more gradually.

Journal Revealings

⬦ Some of the ways I'm beginning to surrender more are . . .

⬦ What my resisting behaviors (habits, patterns) look and feel like when I notice them . . .

◇ What I notice in the present when I needle and feel a difficult situation from my past . . .

◇ Ahas and benefits I'm experiencing as a result of practicing more surrender in my life in general . . .

WEEK 33

Bless and Release

Sorrow is how we learn to love. Your heart isn't breaking. It hurts because it's getting larger. The larger it gets the more love it holds.
—Rita Mae Brown

"Free houseplant. Needs light, love, and a bigger pot."

That's what I wrote on a piece of cardboard and attached to a beloved ficus plant we've had for twenty-two years. Yes, we got her when she was small, the year we moved into our house. And she'd been a beloved member of our family ever since.

The truth is, she needed more light, a bigger pot, and more care than we were able to give her. My hair kept getting snagged in her branches every time I reached around her to open the window shade. She had outgrown our space, and neither my husband nor I could bear the idea of throwing her away.

So we did the best thing we could think of: clean her up, make a big sign, take her out to the curb, snap some photos, and release her with love.

Back in the house, we were pleased to notice that we could still feel her presence. The living room feels completely different in a good way (surprise, surprise). Dare I say, it feels a whole lot airier, brighter, and more spacious. And my hair isn't getting tangled up anymore.

The best part is that in less than five minutes, when we weren't looking, someone swooped in and scooped her up. Who was it? It happened so quickly and stealthily that I've wondered if the ficus gods themselves unburdened her once and for all from us humans who'd held on too long.

Happy endings aside, we all know that most opportunities to practice spacious detachment can be messy. How do we stay present in the face of a deep hurt and move through it?

My answer is and will always be: we have to feel it fully to heal it fully. We need to go all in—into that sometimes scary zone called feeling—and stay there, until something opens and shifts. Here's an example of what this might look like, beautifully articulated by my friend and colleague, Jacob Nordby:

> I woke this morning to find a long, vicious email from someone who has been an important guide and friend for years.
>
> My pattern in the past would be to try to fix this . . . to absorb the pain, understand all sides, make big adjustments, and take responsibility for the lion's share of whatever happened.

I notice today that my internal task is something different.

Today it seems important to go through a private ritual that releases the hurt and allows this other person to feel about or see me as they need to right now.

In other words, I'm not a bulletproof, rugged individualist who doesn't care about what others think of me. I do care. Today I'm challenged to not care less (and not be careless), but to simply allow the medicine to do the work it needs to do—while also letting go of any weight or pain that isn't mine.

For some reason this brings to mind a phrase from Mary Oliver's work:

Someone I loved once gave me a box
full of darkness. It took me years to
understand that this, too, was a gift.

Today I feel the gift now . . . not in some distant future time. Today I can accept the gift of freedom for myself and for this other—freedom from being chained together in a dynamic of pain.

I don't share this to demonstrate that I'm a good person or above it all. In fact, I'm not above it at all. I'm feeling it deeply. What I am grateful for is this ability to let go more quickly of what would otherwise get knotted up inside as pain and invisible weight.

Keyword: freedom.

And if I may add another keyword phrase to Jacob's, it would be this: in present time.

We can only release our burden to the degree that we are in the present moment.

You can practice this by creating a ritual. Because the mind can get so caught up in trying to think its way to a solution, ritual cuts right through the noise and goes straight to the heart. And the sky's the limit on how you can play. As Robert A. Johnson says in his book *Owning Your Own Shadow*:

> You can draw it, sculpt it, write a vivid story about it, dance it, burn something, or bury it—anything that gives expression to that material without doing damage. . . . Remember, a symbolic or ceremonial experience is real and affects one as much as an actual event.

In present time.

Practice

What is something that you have loved or that has served you well that you might be ready to release from your life? What are some ways you can honor it as it is on its way out the door? Use this week to bless and release it by following the steps below.

Blessing and Releasing Process

1. **Identify**: Choose a thing, relationship, belief, or attachment that no longer serves you, feels good, or adds value that you are ready to release.

2. **Connect**: Dust off your anchoring altar (see Week 2), if necessary, and use it to connect with your intention for this clearing. Tune in to the gifts you've received from having this thing, person, or belief in your life.

3. **Release**: Create a ritual that feels good, honors your process of letting go, and expresses gratitude.

4. **Nurture**: Repeat your ritual every day for a week. Notice the sensations that come up as you practice letting go. Take your time with this and notice how it feels before, during, and after.

5. **Reflect**: Record any shifts in your journal—yes, even the tiniest, seemingly most insignificant ones. They matter.

6. **Deepen** (optional): If it resonates and helps, use the spacious clearing process from Week 28 to make it easier to say goodbye to something near and dear.

Journal Revealings

⬦ Something that has served me well and I have loved
that I'm ready to release . . .

⬦ Ways I can ritually honor and bless it as I say goodbye . . .

⬦ What I notice before, during, and after this letting
go process . . .

⬦ What I notice when I express gratitude for the gifts
I've received from having this thing (person, belief)
in my life . . .

WEEK 34

Take the Long View

One could say that going through loss is the great awakener.
It is a potential opening if you don't run away from it. What
is usually condemned as "bad" by the mind and the mind-
made self is actually grace coming into your life.
—Eckhart Tolle

They don't call it heartbreak for nothing. It doesn't matter if it's
the loss of a loved one, a home, a job, a pet, a dream; if it's
expected or it comes on suddenly, it seems we are never, ever
prepared for it. When we go through loss, it feels like the heart

is breaking into a million little pieces. The "potential opening" or "grace" that Eckhart Tolle talks about seems unfathomable.

This is how our daughter felt when she learned that she had not been chosen to receive the full-ride scholarship for which she had been a finalist. With a fifty-fifty chance of winning this award and super positive interviews, it seemed impossible to imagine she wouldn't get it.

And yet, she didn't:

> I didn't get the scholarship. I know setbacks are how we grow as people. I realize this is just another bump in the road. I understand that I am already so blessed to be admitted to these two excellent master's programs. I recognize that I can still excel in grad school, that I'll find a way to pay for it, that I can seek other opportunities for mentorship. But I am still devastated.

It was a tough day for us, too. As her parents and biggest fans, seeing this bright light and extremely hardworking soul experience another hit among so many was a tough one to bear.

She had begun her professional career answering phones as an intern on Capitol Hill (read: no pay), clawed her way up the ladder to become a full legislative assistant (while suffering some blatant gender bias along the way), worked three jobs to pay the rent, powered through graduate entrance exams (multiple times), gotten accepted into several highly competitive master's programs, and become a finalist for the most prestigious scholarship that would provide special mentorship, open doors, and allow her to live debt-free . . .

It really hurt.

After all of the heartbreaking rejections and recoveries we'd witnessed in our young, ambitious daughter's life, it took everything we had not to fall down into the rabbit hole of devastation with her. *How much more could she take?*

This of course meant letting go, again. And digging deep into that reservoir of knowing that things would ultimately work out. They always do, and always have. My email back to her came from that place:

Oh honey! I'm sooooo sorry. You were *so* close.

Let yourself cry and feel the feelings and wonder and not know why . . .

Keep breathing into this and feeling this.

Things are not always what they seem.

Be sad, be mad, get clear . . .

and stay tuned! *It's not over 'til it's over.* There is more yet to be revealed.

Love you!

—Mom

For those of you grieving a painful rejection, hoping for a different outcome, may you find comfort in knowing that we live in a fluid universe. Or, as Thich Nhat Hanh so wisely reminds us, "Thanks to impermanence, everything is possible."

And if it's not a rejection, perhaps there is a different kind of loss or unspeakable sadness you are grieving today. May this message buoy and steady you, too.

May it remind you that there is nothing that light and love and time cannot handle—and heal.

Practice

How do you find your peace when life throws you a major curveball? How do you detach with grace when all you feel is disillusioned, plugged in, . . . *lost?*

The practice this week is a letting go process. The steps below will help you connect with a loss, a hurt, or a wound from your past so that you can embrace, detach from, and heal it. And just to be clear, doing this practice is not about regurgitating a painful memory from your past to make you feel bad. It is designed to help you grow your spacious muscle so that when life throws you a curveball, you have more bandwidth and equanimity to handle it.

Spacious Detachment Process

Note: Before you begin, please review the opening guidelines, centering process (Step 1), and integration process (Steps 10–12) from the Practice in Week 28. Work with this meditation with your eyes open until you have a sense for how it goes, and then take it deeper by practicing with your eyes closed.

1. **Get centered**: Get comfortable. Take an easy breath in and a slow, emptying breath out.

Connect with how you are feeling right now by doing a quick sensory body scan. Keep breathing in and out as you become even more relaxed . . . and present . . . and still.

2. **Recall**: When you feel centered, recall a challenging period or event from your past when you felt stuck, lost, confused, drained, trapped, joyless . . . hopeless. It could be a life dream that didn't materialize the way you'd hoped. It could be a major disappointment, a personal loss or failure, or even a healing crisis. Try to go with your first impulse and don't think too hard.

3. **Put your attention on the tension**: Tune in to the issue with all six of your senses—smell, taste, touch, seeing, hearing, and inner knowing. What does it feel like? What does disappointment, for example, feel like? Or the fact that you were saddled with bills when you had no idea how you were going to pay them? Or that you didn't get into your first choice university or job you were hoping for?

4. **Needle and feel**: Are you aware of any lingering incompletions, unresolved hurts, or loose ends that never got tied up? What does sitting with unfinished business feel like? Keep leaning and breathing into these feelings and allow divine intelligence to do its part.

5. **Pan out**: As you continue to needle and feel the discomfort, imagine that you are a movie camera panning out. Instead of being an actor playing a part in this drama about disappointment, loss, or pain, imagine yourself as an audience member outside the situation, looking in. What does it feel like to look at the situation as a conscious observer *while still feeling deeply* at the same time?

6. **Observe**: Keep panning out and feeling. As you gain more and more distance and perspective, notice the compassion that arises out of this practice (of feeling deeply and detaching at the same time). As you reflect on the experience from this new, wider perch, are you aware of any insights or ahas that are bubbling up? What does it feel like to hang out in this bigger space, leading with spacious detachment?

7. **Release**: When you feel complete, take any lingering issues, unresolved feelings, loose ends, or painful memories that you may still be carrying and let them all go. If it helps, gather every last bit of unpleasant, unfinished stuff into a bundle or a ball like you practiced in Week 28 and release it into the Universe. Watch this ball of stuck energy go up and out, like a balloon, getting farther and farther away from you . . . smaller and smaller . . . until all you see is a little dot . . . and then it is gone.

8. **Refresh and integrate**: Now bring your awareness to your heart and feel its harmonizing presence. Invite it to restore and refresh your entire being with nourishing love and healing light. Thank your heart for the beautiful work it does to remain compassionate and neutral; to hold an unconditional space that makes healing and transformation possible. Ask that it help you stay clear and grounded as you integrate the new frequencies of spacious detachment into your life as you go forward.

9. **Tune in**: Take another nice, easy breath in and a slow, emptying breath out. How does your body feel now? How's your breathing? Your hands: are they warmer . . . tinglier? Do you feel the same or different than when you started? When you feel complete, bring your awareness back to yourself sitting in the room and drink a tall glass of water or two (clearing can be very dehydrating).

10. **Journal**: Jot down your awarenesses from this exercise and deepen your experience by using the prompts below.

Journal Revealings

◇ The challenge I chose to work with was . . .

◇ When I tune in with all of my senses, this challenge feels . . .

◇ What I notice when I lean into the issue and needle it even more . . .

◇ What it feels like to gain distance on this difficult situation while feeling it deeply at the same time . . . (and how it might free me in other ways . . .)

◇ Taking a moment to restore and refresh my entire being feels . . .

◇ What my heart is teaching me about presence and compassion . . .

◇ How I feel now . . .

WEEK 35

Be the Change

Ego says, "Once everything falls into place, I'll feel peace." Spirit says, "Find your peace, and then everything will fall into place."
—Marianne Williamson

No one would argue that the world is out of balance. Many are addicted to excess. Many have lost their way.

No one drives home the evils of consumerism better than Erin Janus in her popular YouTube video, "Get Out of the Materialism Trap Now." She's good. She lays it on thick. Even just watching half of it gets the message across. And yes, it might push a few buttons.

Why would anyone want to watch something that might push their buttons, you might ask?

Here's why: Because buttons are where all the goodies are. Like a freshwater pearl that begins as a simple grain of sand, we cannot become our shimmering, sparkly selves without some level of irritation.

And by that I mean *conscious* irritation, if you want to get technical here.

When you lean into the emotional stuck places in your head and heart, you get the exquisite opportunity to feel them, heal them, and release them once and for all. Yes, it may be painful at times, but there is a really big upside when we open ourselves up safely to the disturbing effects of our world instead of resisting them.

You can practice your spacious detachment by watching a news broadcast that is known for ranting or listening to a talk show where the guests are all shouting over each other.

You can practice by watching Janus's video (available in the Resources section of this book), by taking her message to heart and noticing what your mind does with what you see.

As you watch, remember that racking yourself with guilt over how much stuff or stress you have, judging the unconscious behaviors of your human brothers and sisters, or feeling shame for the abundance of riches you get to enjoy *is not the answer.*

Reactions like these will not create the change you wish to see in the world. Instead, I might suggest another way—a more spacious way—of embracing painful and inconvenient truths:

◇ Focus on what is out of balance in *your* life.

◇ Slow down—with awareness.

◇ Simplify—with awareness.

◇ Feel the feelings with compassionate awareness.

◇ Practice letting go—with compassionate awareness.

◇ Cultivate self-care—with awareness.

◇ Be the change you wish to see.

Does this sound familiar?

If it seems like I'm always repeating myself or saying the same thing a whole bunch of different ways, it's because I am.

You see, until we get the memo that the work of changing the world begins at home—in our own heads and hearts—we need to be reminded.

We need reminding in as many ways as possible what Shakespeare's Hamlet states so clearly: "There is nothing either good or bad, but thinking makes it so."

Practice

What does "Be the change you wish to see in the world" mean to you? What are some small steps you can take this week to embrace some "inconvenient truths"?

The practice this week is twofold.

1. **Embrace:** Notice the painful and inconvenient truths that arise in your life this week. Observe all thoughts and feelings—of anger, resentment, judgment, guilt, shame, worry—without trying to fix or manage them. Repeat the spacious detachment meditation from Week 34 to help you create some space and lighten your load even more.

2. **Get spacious:** Watch Erin Janus's "Get Out of the Materialism Trap Now" (or any video or TV program that rattles your cage just a bit). Watch it with as much spacious detachment as you can. Name and feel the feelings that come up and notice the shifts in you.

Journal Revealings

◇ What I'm noticing when I take a step back from the thoughts and feelings that tend to weigh me down . . .

◇ Thoughts and feelings that arise as I watch a program or video that rattles my cage . . .

◇ Ways that help me soften my resistance . . .

◇ What "Be the change I wish to see" means to me . . .

◇ Small steps that I can take to lighten the load for me and everyone . . .

Persist, Not Resist

Stop resisting.
So much of our anguish is created when we are in
resistance. So much relief, release, and change are
possible when we accept, simply accept.
—Melody Beattie

What happens when you close your eyes and say, "I'm resisting" or "I resist"? What happens when you *feel* into the word itself?

Don't get me wrong—"resist" is not intrinsically a bad word. As a popular political statement, it does not diminish the work of courageous souls declaring their support for peace, equality, and justice in the world. That is not where I'm going with this.

What I mean is that when it comes to being the change we wish to see, resistance does not get us what we want.

Resistance is not going to get us very far when we're trying to clear the insanity in our basements or attics. Nor will it help us diffuse a stressful situation at the office, sort out our finances, or improve the world. Resisting *stops* the flow of energy. It closes the channels to light and healing. It shuts down our ability to change our relationship with whatever it is that is holding us back.

Consider a radiant flower in full bloom. Would it thrive the way it does by resisting growth? Resisting nourishment?

Consider what this student shares in her comment below. Would she be able to discover the spacious wonders of surrender if she didn't get out of her own way?

Something must have shifted in me today, because instead of being all stony and hard-hearted in my ways to get something done and letting fear and anxiety rule my actions, I dared to try a different way.

At various points, instead of getting all fired up, I decided to just be with what is. I chose to listen, notice, and be curious about what was happening. I would wait until the emotion passed—or better yet, until it led me towards some sort of action.

For a few brief moments, I stopped fighting with my life. I slowed down and allowed space between the issue/challenge and the desired outcome.

I surrendered.

Wonder of wonders . . . wildflowers in the form of compassion and gratitude filled me up. Those hard, jagged edges are starting to crumble.

And for all you revolutionaries out there wondering how you can stand your ground, march for what you hold true, and fiercely advocate for what you believe in . . . without resisting: You can start with you. You can quiet the divisive rants going on in your head. You can be a fierce advocate for yourself. You can practice *being* the peace you wish to see.

You can adopt a different word—and modus operandi—that is a lot more powerful, elastic, fluid . . . like resilience.

Can you feel the energetic difference between resistance and resilience?

One small, conscious shift can change everything.

Practice

What are you still resisting?

The focus this week is to notice resisting patterns the minute they arise and use the spacious clearing or detachment meditations you've been practicing from Weeks 28 and 34 to release them. Notice what happens when you question, soften, and surrender the beliefs behind the resisting habits. Notice what happens when you allow these resisting impulses to simply be just another form of stuck energy.

Journal Revealings

◇ What I'm resisting . . .

◇ Why I'm resisting . . .

◇ What I can do to soften resistance as soon as I become aware of it . . .

◇ What happens when I do . . .

Allow Imperfection

Perfectionism is not the same thing as striving to be your best . . . It's a twenty-ton shield that we lug around thinking it will protect us when, in fact, it's the thing that is preventing us from flight.

—Brené Brown

If I were to list some of my imperfections that are rattling my cage at the moment, it would be these:

- ⬦ My new passport photo came out awful. (I will have to live with that face for the next ten years.)

- ⬦ I weeded a flower bed within an inch of its life, and now it looks even worse than it did before. (I will have to look at that gaping hole for the rest of the season and be reminded of how "uncaring" I was.)

- ⬦ I improperly ejected the computer backup drive and screwed it up. (Resolving this problem will require spending time I don't have.)

From the way I've reacted, you'd think my life depended on these things: like no foreign country will let me in for the way I look, or that I'll be sued for garden malpractice, or that all is lost when it comes to technological support.

Are these things worth losing my peace over?

The answer, of course, is no.

No one died. No one got hurt.

It's just that my ego is bruised.

I can be a real terrorist when it comes to myself. I see no compassion, tenderness, or forgiveness in how I hold these realities: no allowing things to be just as they are, such as they are.

And that is because I forgot. I fell into an old habit. I was being unaware.

This is where cycling back to the first three stages of our work—slowing down, simplifying, and sensing—come in superhandy to nudge us to that awareness, to that place of peace, acceptance, and surrender. By taking the time to gently reflect on the sneaky ways we inflict pain on ourselves, we get to feel and heal it. We get to move past the stuckness and into the light.

Speaking of lightening up around our imperfections, there's a really funny video that shows the softening power of imperfection: how it can pierce the "twenty-ton shield" of perfectionism, cut right through its dense and steely veneer, and dissolve it with a flourish. It's called "Children interrupt BBC News interview." You can find the link to it in the back of the book. Enjoy this extra treat and invitation not to take yourself too seriously!

Practice

What are some of your "perfect imperfections" that have been holding you hostage? Are they worth losing your peace over? Would it feel safe to let them go?

The practice this week is to make a list of "mistakes" you're still holding on to and the limiting beliefs lurking behind those imperfections. Notice how slowing down, simplifying, and sensing can help you access and embrace your flaws more easily and what happens when you do.

Journal Revealings

◇ Imperfections and mistakes I've made that make me cringe . . .

◇ Fears about these issues that hold me hostage . . .

◇ Why it is safe for me to soften my resistance and let these go and how it feels when I do . . .

◇ Ways I can lighten up more . . .

WEEK 38

Diminish the Ego, Dissolve the Pain

The ego is not only the unobserved mind, the voice in the head which pretends to be you, but also the unobserved emotions that are the body's reaction to what the voice in the head is saying.
—Eckhart Tolle

I was sitting at a table in a restaurant where my husband and I are regular customers, when the Chinese waiter—a bright light with a perpetual smile, named Philip—came up to welcome me with his signature beam of a smile.

Me? I wasn't feeling the love that day. There was no light, no beaming, no smile. I was bumming out about something, nursing a grudge, in no mood to interact with anyone, especially with a bright-eyed sweetheart of a guy grinning from ear to ear.

But then I heard a whisper, which came through by way of a nudge and a voice in my head that said: *Stephanie, seriously? Get over yourself! Can you just set your little petty drama aside for a sweet second, meet his gaze, and give this man the respect he deserves? Suck it up, sister, and dig deeper. Philip deserves better.*

Thankfully, I listened to my (real) self in that split second. I sucked it up, shoved back my petty little snit of a mood, dug deep, and pulled out as gracious a reply as I could muster.

While it felt awful to kill the switch on my bad mood, which, by the way, was binging on as much negativity as it could, the act itself was surprisingly easy.

As I reached inside myself for a modicum of grace, I noticed Philip reach inside for something too. It was his breast pocket. From it, he pulled out a beautifully embroidered handkerchief and handed it to me. "This is for you," he said. "My wife made it."

Wait, what?

I was stunned, flabbergasted, speechless. Fighting back tears, it took all I had in that moment not to bawl my eyes out for the shame I felt.

We are all wired for basic human kindness and connection. Why is it so easy to forget? What is it about us humans that makes us want to puff ourselves up and hide behind some false front that serves no one, especially ourselves?

Ah yes, that would be the wily ego, that part in all of us that believes it has it all figured out, thinks it's in charge, and is constantly puffing itself up or collapsing.

And who better than master teacher Eckhart Tolle to break it down for us so that we can see the ego for what it really is? In his book *A New Earth,* he shows us the toxic impact that negative thoughts, self-sabotage, and unprocessed pain can have on us and our world and offers a clear pathway through it and into the light.

In short, here's what he says, beginning with the "bad news":

> Any negative emotion that is not fully faced and seen for what it is in the moment it arises does not completely dissolve. It leaves behind a remnant of pain. . . .
>
> The remnants of pain left behind by every strong negative emotion that is not fully faced, accepted, and then let go of join together to form an energy field that lives in the very cells of your body.

Tolle calls this energy field that lives in us the "pain-body." My words for this strong energetic residue (which I share in my first book, *Your Spacious Self*) might be a bit more crass, but they're memorable and hopefully wake us up to our unconscious human habits in the same way. I call this energy field "strings and droppings" ("strings" being the sticky energetic attachments that bind people and things to each other and "droppings" being highly charged stresses we leave behind in our spaces for others to step into or have to process).

When we unconsciously cart around and spew out and "drop" our stringy mess of emotional attachments (unprocessed pain, limiting beliefs, and all those aspects in ourselves that we suppress, resist, or deny), it becomes what Tolle calls "a disease on our planet" that "lives in the collective psyche of humanity."

I would call it simply a toxic mess. Left unchecked, all matter of emotional charge will continue to grow, settle over us like a smog, and affect everything that we care about: our relationships, our living spaces, our world.

I know. *Ouch.*

It may be really messy, but here's the really good news: when we witness emotional pain with compassion and detach from its grip, it releases its charge and dissolves—like magic. It cleans up our internal spaces. It restores balance to our living spaces. It clears the air not just for ourselves, but for everybody. As Tolle says, "It is your conscious Presence that breaks the identification with the pain-body. . . . And when identification with it ceases, the transmutation begins."

What's even more good news is that you've been practicing this way of dissolving old painful patterns since you started this book. *And* you get to deepen your practice of this even more this week.

Yes, you'll have less fake stuff to puff up.

That, my friends, is freedom.

Practice

What would happen if you stopped feeding the ego with beliefs and behaviors that make it feel superior or inferior? What would happen to your sense of self if you spent a week observing instead of reacting? What would it feel like to rest deeply in knowing that you are way bigger and more powerful than the ego self?

The practice this week is to surrender even more: let the hot air out of the ego and give your spacious self room to expand. You'll do this by cultivating active non-doing (not reacting). Watch what happens when you simply allow yourself to feel the burn of an injustice, for example, or the discomfort of not being heard, without doing anything to fix or manage the situation.

Tolle gives us an excellent primer for how to diminish the ego in *A New Earth:*

> A powerful spiritual practice is consciously to allow the diminishment of ego when it happens without attempting to restore it. . . . For example, when someone criticizes you, blames you, or calls you names, instead of immediately retaliating or defending yourself—do nothing. Allow the self-image to remain diminished and become alert to what that feels like deep inside you. For a few seconds, it may feel uncomfortable, as if you had shrunk in size. Then you may sense an inner spaciousness that feels intensely alive. You haven't been diminished at all. In fact, you have expanded. . . .

Another aspect of this practice is to refrain from attempting to strengthen the self by showing off, wanting to stand out, be special, make an impression, or demand attention. It may include occasionally refraining from expressing your opinion when everybody is expressing his or hers, and seeing what that feels like.

Wherever you feel most puffed up, activated, or diminished—be it with family, with coworkers, or on social media—would be the perfect place to start your practice this week.

Journal Revealings

◇ Some of the ways I tend to react when someone criticizes me . . .

◇ What it feels like when I observe the criticism instead of reacting to it . . .

◇ What I'm noticing about myself when I refrain from calling attention to myself . . .

◇ If I were to give my ego self a name, it would be . . .

Claim and Receive

The turning point: When the priority switches from
enriching, to being enriched. A powerful moment.
—Hugh McLeod

Channel surfing the other night landed me on *The Da Vinci Code* starring Tom Hanks—the movie based on Dan Brown's best-selling book.

What affected me about this movie wasn't the nighttime chase scenes, the cavernous Louvre and its bloody parquet floors, the ancient secret rituals, the creepy albino killer, the claustro-phobic Harvard professor and his pretty doe-eyed French companion, the big puzzle that kept getting bigger, Michelangelo's masterpieces, or even the idea (spoiler alert) of Mary Magdalene as Jesus's wife.

What affected and surprised me about this movie was less about a thing or a person, a lesson or a bloodline, than a deeper inquiry of the Holy Grail itself, as interpreted by Dan Brown's Professor Robert Langdon, here:

"[L]egend tells us the Holy Grail is a chalice—a cup. But the Grail's description as a *chalice* is actually an allegory to protect the true nature of the Holy Grail. . . .

"The Grail is literally the ancient symbol for womanhood, and the *Holy* Grail represents the sacred feminine and the goddess, which of course has now been lost, erased by the Church. The power of the female and her ability to produce life was once very sacred, but it posed a threat to the rise of a Church headed by men. It was man, not God, who created the concept of Original Sin, whereby Eve tasted of the apple in the Garden of Eden and caused the downfall of the human race. Woman, once the sacred giver of life, became the enemy."

It got me thinking bigger questions, like what would it feel like for us humans to fully embody the receptive, feminine part of ourselves—to accept, allow, listen, soften, trust, embrace, flow, feel, not know, let go, soften, surrender, remember?

What would it take to reclaim the part of ourselves that has been lost by "his-story" and separation thinking?

How big do we want to be, and how much more love, nourishment, ease, support, abundance, pleasant surprises are we willing to receive? Because from a quantum perspective, the sky's the limit.

I may not have all the answers yet to these big questions. What I do know is that so many wars have been fought to tamp down our divine human bigness and our innate wisdom. I also know that the tide is changing. The feminine is back. She's not only nourishing, she's a badass warrior that is showing us a *whole* other way to be.

She's showing us that for us to clear old patterns that are holding us back, claim our true spacious selves, and be the change we wish to see in the world, we must slow down and simplify, sense and surrender, and cultivate self-care.

Yes, this sounds like the five steps to spaciousness—all feminine ways of being.

Practice

What would it feel like to fully embody your true self? What gets in your way of fully claiming your spacious power and receiving the blessings and abundance that come with it?

The practice this week is twofold.

1. **Claim**: Imagine what it feels like to fully claim and embody your spacious power. Reflect on this powerful person that you are becoming and *feel into it* deeply and completely—all the way down to your bones.

2. **Receive**: Reflect on the abundance, blessings, and nourishment you would like to receive more of in your life and what it would feel like to receive them.

Use the prompts that follow to help you open up. Take them with you into your day. Reflect on them in your journal. Live them.

And P.S., if my story from *The Da Vinci Code* is confusing you as it relates to this week's lesson, that would be an example of something getting in your way. Use it to practice letting go and get on with living your life and claiming what truly matters.

Journal Revealings

◇ What spacious power means to me . . .

◇ What would happen if I fully allowed myself to expand into and embody my true self . . .

◇ What I'd like to receive more of . . .

◇ What I am willing to do to receive more blessings, abundance, and nourishment in my life . . .

WEEK 40

Get Light

A good day is a good day. A bad day is a good story.
At the end of the day, it's all good.
—Glennon Doyle

Airplane rides. We've all been on them. Unfortunately, what we most focus on these days are the hassles: the packing, going through security, making our connections, getting home on time.

We have totally lost touch with the true marvel of sitting in a chair at 36,000 feet above sea level, hurtling through space at 500 miles per hour without as much as a hair getting out of place.

I mean seriously. How amazing is *that!?*

Unless there is another plane in the sky to give you some perspective, it feels like you're virtually crawling like a snail to your destination.

But of course we all know we're not.

Moving about your life in the slow lane is no different.

Next time you feel like you're moving at a glacial pace, getting nowhere, falling off the wagon, losing hope, going three steps forward and four back, remember the plane ride.

What is really happening—under the radar of any discernible progress—is quite the opposite from what your mind is telling you.

When you focus your intention, set doable action steps, let go of attachment to the outcome, and nourish yourself with self-care—*every day*—you are, in fact, traveling at the speed of light.

Practice

What is shifting in your world—inside and out? In what ways are you more capable of surrendering?

Use this week to reflect on the past forty weeks and what they have been like for you. Go through your journal and highlight your biggest shifts, takeaways, and ahas. Notice how far you've traveled on this journey—especially if it doesn't feel like much has changed.

Journal Revealings

⬦ Ways that I feel more light and spacious since I began this journey forty weeks ago . . .

⬦ Major (and minor) shifts that are taking place in my world right now . . .

⬦ Ways that I have shown myself capable of surrendering . . .

⬦ What really matters to me now (versus forty weeks ago) . . .

PART 5

SELF-CARE

*drink from the well
of your self
and begin
again.*
—Charles Bukowski

It's all well and good to dial it down, feel our feelings to their full and natural completion, and detach from outcomes. But if we don't feel safe in the process, we will not budge an inch. We will react and contract. This is where nourishing self-care comes into the picture and plays a big part in our clearing journey.

Self-care is the container of safety, the softening balm of clearing. It means making choices that honor our true nature, setting clear boundaries with others (even if it disappoints them), telling the truth about our experience, and being fierce advocates for ourselves.

As we turn the corner on the final twelve weeks of this book, our primary focus will be on the fifth S—self-care. We will examine ways to turn up the light even more, explore more of what it means to claim our true selves, and connect the five S's to each other on our path to spacious wholeness.

WEEK 41

Nourish and Flourish

Be kinder to yourself. And then
let your kindness flood the world.
—Pema Chödrön

There's a photo I took that always cracks me up when I see it. It's of someone I don't know, standing with her friends at an outdoor wedding reception. Like everyone with her, she's totally glammed up—hair, makeup, gown. She's dressed to the nines, save for one thing. Her shoes. Underneath that gown, she's wearing a pair of white hotel slippers.

Well, duh! Who needs high heels when you can wear slippers instead, right?

All kidding aside, what I love about the picture is how it epitomizes what it means to put ourselves first:

◇ To choose radical self-care over trying to impress or
do the right thing.

◇ To choose ease over effort.

◇ To choose "no" or "doesn't work for me" over "should."

◇ To choose simplicity over complication.

◇ To choose letting go over holding on.

◇ To choose joy over pain.

Why would we want to choose anything else?

And yet, still, we continue to choose everything but ourselves.

What are some of the ways you tend to cut yourself short and settle for less than you deserve? For example, do you hold back from requesting a better table at a restaurant (seat on a plane, room at a hotel) because you just don't want to "trouble" anyone (read: *I don't want to be rejected*)? Do you defer to "more capable" colleagues at work when given a chance to weigh in or voice an opinion because "they know more than I do," or "they just seem to want it more" (read: *I don't want risk being seen and heard*)? Do you remain silent when you are served a meal that is too cold, underdone, or not what you ordered because it's much easier to "keep things simple" and not rock the boat (read: *I don't feel deserving*)?

If so, let this be your week to reverse this pattern and choose *you* instead. Let these words by Anaïs Nin wash over you and help you get started:

And the day came when the risk to remain tight in a bud was more painful than the risk it took to blossom.

You've got plenty of "buds." It's time now to let them open and blossom!

Practice

What are some of the ways you shortchange yourself? What would it take for you to put yourself first? What is one thing you'd like to step into and declare that honors you?

The practice this week is twofold.

1. **Reflect**: Take some time in your journal to reflect on the ways you unnecessarily defer, tolerate, or settle for less. Write down anything and everything you can think of where you might tend to "choose other" over you so as not to create conflict and feel your feelings. Notice what it feels like in your body as you download. Notice your thoughts. Notice your breathing. Bring as much self-kindness and compassion to this process as you can. When you feel complete, let it all go. Shake it all out and do something that feels really good and nourishing.

2. **Give yourself permission**: As you go about your day, bring spacious awareness to the choices you make around self-care. Lean into any discomfort you might feel when you put yourself first in situations where you would normally defer. Give

yourself permission to disappoint others who
may not understand or even like this "new you."
(Remember, it's all practice.)

Journal Revealings

◇ Ways that I shortchange myself . . .

◇ Ways I am inclined to defer so as not to create
unnecessary conflict . . .

◇ What it feels like to open up and blossom . . .

◇ Beginning now, I declare that I will no longer . . .

◇ Beginning now, I choose this for me . . .

WEEK 42

Put the Self in Self-Care

*Radical self-care is quantum, and radiates out into the
atmosphere, like a little fresh air. It is a huge gift to the world.*
—Anne Lamott

Self-care—we all know it's good for us, but what does it mean,
and what does it really look like in practice?

For *Posts from the Path* blogger Tyler Lewke, it can be simple
and sweet, like this:

I began to investigate what being kind to myself and having more self care might look like. I did simple things like moving my phone out of my bedroom, deleting Facebook from the phone and buying an alarm clock that has no sound but uses light to mimic the sunrise. Will and I have found some amazing new hikes. My food is healthier, I even take a couple vitamins now. My journal has more words in it. My house is cleaner.

For best-selling author Anne Lamott, self-care is more radical, and revolutionary, as she shares in a piece for *Spirituality & Health*:

Radical self-care means that I gently bust myself out of the desperate lifelong need to please, and it means that I start to say no as a complete sentence. . . . Without radical self-care I'm like some demented flight attendant and they're first-class travelers.

Lamott doesn't stop there. Here is the clincher on what's *really* happening under the surface of our need to please:

In a very paradoxical, pathetic, natural way, we calm ourselves by worrying about others. And obsessing about others keeps us out of our own worry. Black-belt codependents like me use other people as a drug to keep from having to deal with our own aloneness or feelings or care about the world, so that instead of thinking about global warming, you can think about your children's swim lessons—we think it's all more manageable. The fact is, it keeps us stoned and worried in obsession.

As for me, I see self-care as both sweet, revolutionary, *and* basic to our survival. It is as essential to our well-being as breathing.

In other words, it's not optional.

There's definitely the yummy, feel-good side. I mean, really, who doesn't love taking a break over a cup of tea? Or getting a massage once in a while?

But there is also the badass side, as in being an advocate for yourself. It means giving yourself massive amounts of slack when you mess up and telling the truth about your experience. It means setting clear boundaries with others and potentially disappointing them when you say no, like this student does here with her friend:

A friend called to ask if I could tailor a bedroom outfit for her. She had bought a quilt and extra shams and knew I quilted. Could I make the quilt larger, then make some unique pillows to complement them? Luckily, I knew that my schedule couldn't accommodate any of that, so I truly thanked her for thinking of me and gave her the name and number of a tailor I know who does excellent work. By saying no to her I said a huge YES to me. Still patting myself on the back to my own self-care. Just because I'm able doesn't mean I need to validate my strengths in that arena by stretching myself too thin. *Ahhh,* yes to life and feeling fine.

The best part of folding self-care into a daily routine is that it effectively rewires the brain and becomes habit-forming. It transforms your association of "life is hard" into the feeling of life as delicious and fun! This can be especially useful when combined with tasks that you find more onerous, like clutter clearing. Yes, you just might have the urge to purge because of how good it feels—not because of some "should" game your mind has been playing.

For us to feel lighter and more spacious, we must change the paradigm of self-neglect. And the best way I know to do that is to slow down and simplify, sense and surrender.

Name the pain, feel it, release it, repeat.

So, what is one thing you can do today that would support you and feel really good? That would be a good place to start. And repeat it again tomorrow. And the next day . . . and the next . . . until it becomes habit-forming.

Practice

What needs to happen for you to change the paradigm of self-neglect?

The practice this week is twofold.

1. **Feel good**: Insert at least five conscious minutes of self-care into your day. It can be as simple as listening to a piece of beautiful music, drinking tea out of your favorite teacup, or sitting by an open window and feeling the breeze on your face. Notice if this one action expands into more desire to feel good and more moments that bring you joy.

2. **Reflect**: Take some time to reflect on what self-care means to you in your journal.

Journal Revealings

⬦ What self-care means to me and why it matters . . .

⬦ Why I know that self-care is not optional . . .

⬦ One thing I can do for at least five minutes every day this week that supports me . . .

⬦ What it feels like to consistently nourish myself . . .

Choose You

Don't go see someone who is irritating. Take a day off from work if you feel tired. Go to the beach if it calls you. Listen to more of the music that pleases you. Soothe yourself in any way that you can.

Let your mantra be, "Today, no matter where I'm going and no matter what I'm doing, it is my dominant intent to please myself. . . . I'm going to be nicer to me.
—Abraham-Hicks

Last winter and spring I was fried. I had given everything I had to write, birth, and launch my second book, and I had nothing left to give. I was sure I had more in me to say—I just wasn't feeling it. I was running on empty.

In the absence of motivation and juice, I reached for the one thing that has always given me joy: my camera.

I dusted off my Instagram account, pushed through my resistance to figure out how the platform worked, and started to reconnect with one of my very first loves: taking pictures.

I set a simple intention to post one photo a day. It was so much fun opening myself up to whatever I might encounter: it could be the way the afternoon light danced through a window, or a grove of trees pulling me in and speaking to me in their magic tree language.

I had no ultimate goal, no attachment to the outcome, no need to post the perfect photo. This daily exercise was not about pleasing anyone but myself. It was just me, my camera, and my world.

What this one simple devotional act led to over the course of two years was nothing short of miraculous. In fact, it inspired this book. It gave me new eyes to see, more bandwidth to receive, and a renewed clarity of purpose that I thought I'd used up birthing my previous books and projects.

Back when I was researching the subject of happiness in women for my second book, I came across the work of Marcus Buckingham. He's the author of *Find Your Strongest Life: What the Happiest and Most Successful Women Do Differently,* a book that explores why today's women are less happy than they were forty years ago.

Though the points he makes below (with *highlights* by me for emphasis) can seem more academic than practical, they definitely got me thinking. According to Buckingham, the happiest and most successful women . . .

◇ Don't agonize over who they aren't—they *accept and act on* who they are. They have discovered the role they were born to play and they play it.

◇ Don't juggle—they catch-and-cradle. They don't keep things at bay, but *select a few things* and draw them in close.

⬦ Don't strive for balance—they *strive for fullness*. They intentionally imbalance their lives toward those moments that make them feel strong.

⬦ Always sweat the small stuff—they know and *act on* the specific details of *what invigorates them* (and they let go of what doesn't strengthen them).

What the research suggests, in a nutshell, is that successful women—and men too—make space for themselves. They don't expect to do it all or get it perfect. They simply zero in on what serves and supports them, and they act on it.

That pretty much summarizes my process too, which I'll share in greater detail in next week's lesson.

I would also add that without the five S's working their good juju on me, this book would definitely not exist.

Practice

What pleases you? How can you have more of what pleases you? What gets in your way of doing what pleases you?

The practice this week is to make space for yourself: select a few things that you love doing, and act on them. Start by listing the things in your journal that make your heart sing, and notice the stories you tell yourself about *why it's just not possible* to have, do, or be these things. Anytime you feel a gulp or a pang of resistance (you'll know by how it feels in your body), give it some space. Use the awareness tools you've been learning to dissolve it.

Strive for progress, not perfection.

Journal Revealings

◇ What pleases me the most . . .

◇ What I can do this week to have more of what pleases me . . .

◇ Some of my worries about doing what I most enjoy (if I'm being totally honest) . . .

◇ What it feels like to act on these desires . . .

WEEK 44

Honor Your Process

Every time we say YES because we're afraid of missing out, we say no to something. That something may be a big dream or a short nap. We need both. Courage to stay our course and gratitude for our path will keep us grounded and guide us home.
—Brené Brown

Last week I shared my story of running on empty and doing the only thing that could help me move through my stuckness, which, at the time, was to make art.

What I didn't share is all the behind-the-scenes "clearing" I had to do to heal some vulnerabilities and unworthiness issues I was feeling around putting my work out in the world. Taking pictures was one thing; sharing them publicly was another. Stretching myself in this way was beginning to kick up some good old juicy fears I had around being seen in this new way.

What my year of posting pictures taught me is that for me to heal from these old fears of showing up and being seen, I needed to needle and feel them with compassion and awareness until they lost their grip on me. I also needed to get really clear on what matters to me and advocate for it.

If I were to break down in detail what advocating for myself and making room for what matters looks like for me now, it would be something like this:

The first way is that I make it a priority to cultivate my passion. For example:

⬦ I make the time. I choose my muse over other things that don't feel so joyful.

⬦ I guard my time. I don't let other things squeeze out my love of taking pictures or writing when I'm inspired to write. It's really important that I not allow my inspiration to get away from me, because I know once it's gone, it's gone.

⬦ I don't push it. I back off when I'm not inspired or in the mood. I'll do other things and wait until I get the signal to dive in again.

⬦ I give myself permission. As a person who tries to keep her word, I recognize that things can change, so I give myself permission to change my mind. I create and adjust, like the other day when I had planned to FaceTime with a dear friend while in the throes of an inspiration. I emailed her and asked to postpone our chat: *Nancy, I can't talk today . . . I've got to ride this wave.*

◇ I say no. If something feels like a "should" or doesn't feel right, I graciously decline by saying something like, *Sorry, it doesn't work for me.*

◇ I put attention to the tension. When my old fear patterns around sharing my art (being seen) start to kick up, I give them as much compassionate space as I can. I stop, breathe, observe, and feel the queasy vulnerabilities until they ease.

The second way I advocate for myself is that I feed and nurture the passion every single day. For example:

◇ When I need a "beauty boost" (which is about every day), I go visual: I fill myself up by scrolling through magazines, my Instagram feed, or my favorite boards on Pinterest featuring beautiful homes and gardens, DIY tips, and inspirational quotations.

◇ I follow Instagramers who are doing high-level work and unfollow anyone who starts ranting or is noisy and negative.

◇ I listen to jazz every night. We have an ad-free station that we turn on when we're making dinner.

◇ I read books about the creative process, like *Big Magic* by Elizabeth Gilbert, and inspiring memoirs by women who've pushed through huge obstacles to follow their dreams, like Gloria Steinem and Patti Smith.

◇ I watch TV shows that nurture my artistic spirit, like *Chef's Table* (see Week 25), or shows that feature talent so good and so moving it makes me cry, like *So You Think You Can Dance.*

That pretty much sums up my process. And when I get stuck or lost, I simply loop back to the beginning—back to slowing down and simplifying, sensing and surrendering—to help me find my way again.

Practice

How do you make room for what matters in your life? What simple tweaks or improvements can you make, and what happens when you do?

The practice this week is twofold.

1. **Focus on what matters**: Continue where you left off last week, and make space for what matters to you and refine your process so that it happens. And if you have a tendency to say yes because of a deep fear of missing out

(FOMO), use this week to needle and feel your FOMO tendencies and reverse the pattern by choosing differently: only say yes to *you* and notice the space you create in doing so.

2. **Focus on progress, not perfection**: Adopt as your mantra this quote by twentieth-century French psychologist Dr. Emile Coué: "Every day, in every way, I am getting better and better." Notice what happens when you repeat it daily.

Journal Revealings

◇ What matters most to me is . . .

◇ Ways that I make room for what matters . . .

◇ Adjustments I can make to improve my process . . .

◇ Ways that I act out my fears of missing out . . . (and what I notice when I make conscious choices that honor me instead . . .)

◇ Ways that I know I am getting better and better . . .

Step In, Step Back, Step Up

Boundaries, boundaries, boundaries.
Don't leave home without them . . .
—Jeff Brown

Boundaries—we touched upon them in Week 42. How do we separate from our need to fix, manage, and help others, when everything we've been taught is to step in, give of ourselves, and *help*?

Here's what I know: For us to truly be able to shine brightly and exercise spacious detachment in ways that are real and don't fry our circuits, we need to set boundaries—even if doing so means disappointing others and letting go of our need to be liked and approved of.

Here's what setting clear boundaries can look like:

◇ Being a fierce advocate for ourselves

◇ Saying no when we mean no

◇ Establishing what's okay and acceptable and what is unacceptable or not okay

◇ Honoring our innate wisdom

◇ Allowing our feelings to guide us

Though it may not feel like it, or come easily at first, setting clear boundaries is a high act of generosity and integrity on your part for another. It's a paradigm shift in our thinking and requires consistent, mindful tending.

Still, this begs the question: Just how do we step into a situation without stepping out of our selves in the process? This is where your practice of the five S's becomes your lifeline.

To illustrate, let's say you've made it very clear to your teenage son that he must return from his Saturday night date by 11 p.m. sharp and the family car must be returned in the condition that he found it.

At midnight, Junior saunters in, slumps in front of the TV, and leaves the car littered with Burger King wrappers and no gas.

Clearly a boundary has been crossed.

Here's how applying the five S's can help you support yourself. Use them to process your experience of the situation *before* confronting the issue or jumping to conclusions:

1. **Slow down**: Take a deep breath before talking to your son. It will help you calm down and get clear. Giving yourself this time will help you recall the agreement you made with him. For example, were you really clear about the return time? Did you make it clear that he should return the car with gas? Once you've calmed down, notice which boundaries got crossed and how you're prepared to deal with them.

2. **Simplify**: Simplifying means keeping your focus strictly on accountability for the current situation, *not* dredging up previous violations. Simplifying also means following through with the next three steps.

3. **Sense**: Bring your full awareness to how you are feeling in this moment. How's your breathing? Are you feeling tight? Whatever it is that you're experiencing—whether it is waffly, or passive-aggressive, or simmering rage—notice what these emotions *feel like* and where you feel them. Allow the discomfort to bubble up. After about a minute of tuning in, come back to your breathing and notice if it has changed.

4. **Surrender**: Take a step back and notice the drama playing out in your home and heart as if it were a movie you are watching. This is where you continue to feel the emotions—the wafflyness, passive-aggressiveness, or pissed-off-ness—but in a more detached and witnessing way. Observing in this way includes self-judgment. If you can't yet get to this stage, return to Step 3, or 2, or 1—your breathing— whichever step feels appropriate at this moment.

5. **Self-Care**: Give yourself space and slack to feel whatever comes up for you. Remind yourself that it's okay and safe to be uncomfortable; being a parent is messy sometimes; you are the adult here, and your job ultimately is to keep your son safe. And

P.S., it is *your* car, after all, not his, and he has just
lost the privilege of using it until further notice.

Cycle through these stages as many times as necessary until
you start to feel centered and grounded. From this more spacious place you'll be able to talk to your son in a way that honors
your integrity and his. And guess what? He may even listen and
do better next time.

Further, it's okay if the situation continues to be messy for a
while—but you won't be.

A final note about this process: it's important to remember
that these steps don't necessarily happen in the exact sequence
that they are presented here. While slowing down and simplifying might be the two logical places to start, you will begin to
notice a natural fusion between sensing and surrendering as well.
Over time, all five S's—which are designed to work together to
bring you back into balance—will become a seamless flow.

You'll also notice that the more you master the Spacious
Way of setting clear boundaries, the easier it will be. Buttons
won't get as pushed as much, challenges will clear more quickly
and easily, and you'll start to feel the effortless magic of being in
the flow of your life.

Practice

Is there a boundary that has been violated or crossed that could
use some clearing? Is there a challenging someone or something at
home or at work that isn't sitting well or that has violated your trust?

Use this week to bring awareness to a boundary that has been crossed and apply the five steps to process the situation. Keep cycling through each of the steps—both in your journal and in your life—until the emotional charge you've been carrying begins to ease. If it helps, do another round with the spacious clearing and detachment meditations in Weeks 28 and 34.

Journal Revealings

◊ Something that is bothering me, challenging me, does not sit well, has violated my trust . . .

◊ What happens when I apply the five S's to this issue . . .

◊ The S (or S's) that could use more of my attention and practice . . .

◊ Ahas and discoveries I'm making about this process . . .

WEEK 46

Create Your Sanctuary

Stay, stay at home, my heart, and rest.
Home-keeping hearts are happiest.
—Henry W. Longfellow

It doesn't matter if you live in a sprawling mansion surrounded by an old-growth forest or a tiny apartment overlooking the town dump—if your spirit feels nourished and held, lifted and light, consider yourself blessed.

You can argue that it helps to have good raw materials to work with: a good location, good bones, good juju. Still, creating a nourishing nest or landing pad isn't solely dependent on what you luck into, inherit, or can buy. A clear and spacious home is something that you fundamentally attract and cultivate by being clear and spacious yourself.

Ultimately, it is the conscious infusions of love, light, and laughter that transform a house that *you live in* into a home that *lives in you.*

So what does a soulful communion between home and self look and feel like, exactly? For author Elizabeth Gilbert, creating a space to nurture her passion for writing, for example, is quite simple. It begins with a small space, a beloved desk, and several carefully chosen objects to inspire and remind her of what matters. In this excerpt from her Facebook page, she walks us through it:

> I love this room, which is just the right size for me— only a little bit bigger than my beloved old desk. (In fact, I built the room around the desk, so that it can never be removed. Kind of like Odysseus's bed.) . . .
>
> There on the right is my favorite lamp, which looks like a sail. (It reminds me to be free.)
>
> There, beneath the lamp, is the emblem from my first car—a 1966 Plymouth Fury II, that I bought for

600 dollars and drove all the way to Wyoming by myself when I was 23 years old. (It reminds me to be brave.)

Also, there's a plant. (It reminds me to be alive.)

Also, there's a robin's egg. (It reminds me to be vulnerable.) . . .

The spaces that we make for ourselves in which to be quiet and creative MATTER. They don't have to be big rooms. It can be just a little corner, like this room. But the space should be clean, and everything in that space should remind you of who you are. There should be nothing in that space that doesn't bring your senses to life.

Though no less intentional, my approach to creating a sanctuary veers more toward the sensory than the symbolic. Take my home altar, for example. It has morphed more times than I can count; it changes like the seasons, depending on my mood and what shows up in my life.

It started with a "shabby chic" chest that I bought on sale at Marshalls. Above it, I hung a framed wooden shelf made to look old, with a painting of an angel inside. It reminds me of Mexico, where I was born and raised. Like siblings from different parents, the chest and the shelf look like they were made to go together.

I wanted something alive and green in that space, so I placed a plant inside a brass planter that has been in my family for years.

The salt lamp came next, which I love for its cleansing properties and warm glow at night.

Save for a few small, random objects that I placed inside the wooden shelf—a Chinese medallion for good luck and abundance, a small Tibetan prayer wheel, and a couple of beautiful notecards featuring birds—I was not moved to add anything else.

That is, I wasn't until the amazing quartz birds came into our lives that our Brazilian housepainter gifted us (see Week 23). While I loved the pieces, two was way too many to display in this small space, so I picked the taller one: the parrot, which I propped up using a little rustic box that I repurposed.

This space makes my heart sing every time I walk by it. It will no doubt change again and again over time. What I find so interesting about my communion with this space is that while I love birds, I never consciously set out to create an altar to them! But there it is.

Maybe you're not there yet. Maybe you're far from being able to carve out a clean little sanctuary nook for yourself, let alone know what matters to you. How do you bridge the gap?

You can start by weeding out the things that no longer spark joy and letting in the things that do. As Melissa Camara Wilkins says in her article "10 Things Minimalists Don't Do":

> The things you're surrounded by remind you of what you believe is important. If you don't weed out the belongings you've outgrown, it's like your past is living with you all the time. You don't need to own everything you've ever used. Keep things that support who you are, who you're becoming, and let go of the rest.

As we explored in Week 12, some things can spark joy when we move them around. Before you discard an item you have loved, I might suggest you place it somewhere else, or weed out what's around it, and use your intuition to see if the joy is still there. If not, discard it with love and gratitude for what the object has meant to you and move on.

In the end, raising the energy in a space is a continuous process. To the degree that you're willing to play with your spaces and keep things moving is what makes for a happy home.

Practice

What would make your home feel more like a sanctuary? What are some ways you can infuse your home with a little more love, light, and laughter? If your home could talk, what would it say to you?

To help you home in, take some time every day this week to commune with it. Use the steps below to turn it into a safe, nourishing haven.

Creating a Home Sanctuary

1. **Choose a space**: Begin with one room to commune with . . . or a smaller area, a closet, a drawer, or whatever moves you. Start slow. Keep it simple.

2. **Sense**: Do a full sensory scan of the space. Notice your breathing.

3. **Check in**: Say hello. Ask the space what it needs to feel more "loved up" and supported and wait for the answer.

4. **Make adjustments**: Move things around, if necessary, or do a little weeding to help you zero in on objects that spark joy.

5. **Fine-tune**: Add something that lights you up, supports you, or represents who you are or who you are becoming.

6. **Bless and move on**: When you feel the "click" of completion register in your heart, thank your space, bless it, and move on to another.

Journal Revealings

◇ What it feels like to commune with each space of my home . . .

◇ Spaces in my home that feel good . . .

◇ Objects in my home that spark joy . . .

◇ Ways that I can "love up" my home even more . . .

◇ Changes that would make a difference in how I feel "at home" in my home . . .

Remember What Lights You Up

I am out with lanterns, looking for myself.
—Emily Dickinson

Here's what I'm wondering: Did you take the time last week to commune with your home? Did you have fun finding new ways to create a nourishing sanctuary for yourself?

Or did you blow the whole thing off?

In fact, how many of these lessons are you skimming or skipping? Are you just giving them a little cursory scan and moving on with life as usual?

I'm telling you this not to make you feel bad, or guilty, or shamed. (Although if it brings up some squirmy resistance, you have the perfect opportunity to embrace and dissolve it.)

No, my purpose is simply to act as your nudgy higher self and remind you what you signed up for this year.

To remind you that ultimately this book is not about me, or the lessons, or what you did or didn't do with the lessons.

It's about *you.*

It's about how much you are willing to invest in yourself. How much of *you* you are willing to put before something or someone else.

It's about remembering what you love and cultivating more of it.

To that end, if you could use a little gentle assist in remembering why you're here, below is a simple, fun tool that can bring you back. It's another goodie inspired by author Elizabeth Gilbert. I call it the "remembering jar." Here's what you need for it to work:

⬦ A big jar, box, basket, or container

⬦ Bits of paper on which you write down happy highlights of your day, every day

⬦ Your willingness to play

What lights you up? What IS working in your life? What makes you feel peaceful, easeful, joyful? Write it down and place it in the jar so you'll remember when you need it most. It will be your mirror and your best friend.

Next time you feel discouraged or lost, like you're floundering or buried in chaos, take a moment to reach inside the jar and pull out a nugget of hope and inspiration.

The jar will help you *remember,* in the best and truest sense of the word, which means to call back and gather all of our scattered parts. It's also a beautiful way to combine all five S's you've practiced this year.

Speaking of remembering, do you remember the anchoring altar you created way back in Week 2? It was an invitation to create a safe, nourishing nook or space in your home that would serve as your home base; a place where you could anchor your intentions, quiet the mind, and feed your spirit.

Do you still have one? Do you still use one? Does it support you?

If not, I might suggest a revisit of that lesson. You are definitely not the same person you were when you began this book. Having a dedicated sacred space for you to retreat and find your center could be more powerful and meaningful to you now.

Practice

What is it that you would like to remember most when it matters most?

The practice this week is twofold.

1. Create a remembering jar: Get yourself a beautiful jar or container, put it in a place that you will see, and populate it with spacious feelings, memories, and successes that lift you up and lighten your load. Jot down some of the joys, shifts, or spacious reveals and place them inside the jar. It could be the unexpected compliment you received, or the awesome feeling you got from folding your clothes and clearing your closet last weekend, or the memory of your favorite pie coming out of the oven and how it made you feel safe and good . . . It could be the fact that you reached a milestone by completing forty-seven weeks of this book! Keep this remembering process going for a year, and notice how it supports your practice of the five S's.

2. Revisit your anchoring altar: Go back to Week 2 and reread the practice. If you don't have or use a home base for yourself, you may want to consider creating one now. If you do have one, you might want to check in and see if it is serving you as well as it could. Maybe it could use a little refresh of objects or an updating of intentions. Use the steps from last week's lesson on creating a home sanctuary to connect with and revitalize it. If, on the other hand, your anchoring altar is not working for you, is just taking up space and gathering dust, this would be a good opportunity to release it with love and make room for something that matters.

Journal Revealings

◇ What lights me up . . .

◇ What is working in my life these days . . .

◇ Other thoughts, feelings, and memories that I'd like to place in my remembering jar . . .

◇ Ways that an anchoring altar can be useful to me now . . .

WEEK 48

Bow to Joy

Unless you leave room for serendipity how can the divine enter in?
—Joseph Campbell

When was the last time you were surprised by something that made you go, *wait, what?!*

Or you saw something totally unexpected that made you laugh out loud?

Or you had an experience that made no sense at all but you loved it anyway and it shifted the energy of your day?

All of that happened to me recently. I was taking my afternoon walk and I heard a fast-tempo trumpet sound getting closer and closer. With no idea what it might be, I pulled out my phone and put it on video mode in the hopes that maybe it would be something really delightful. And it was!

What literally breezed by was a shirtless bike rider wearing a crazy hat, flying a kite, and playing a trumpet—all at the same time.

Wait, what?!

I know. And as if that weren't enough, he took a bow when he saw me. I hadn't noticed the bow part until I watched the video later that day. For a split second it felt like he was my court jester, reminding me not to take anything too seriously.

Strange occurrences that make no sense (and perfect sense at the same time) are some of the ways light reveals itself. In my experience, this is the kind of thing that starts to happen a lot more when you adopt a daily diet of the five S's.

What is one thing about yourself that you take way too seriously that could be lightened up? What is something serious you've been holding on to—a thought, a worry, a fear—that could be switched out and replaced with its opposite? What is one thing that you can do to insert some unmitigated joy into your day today?

Let's find out.

In JOY!

Practice

What unexpected pleasures reveal themselves to you when you lighten up? As an energy, what does "serious" feel like, and how does it compare to the energy of joy? What does pessimism do to your energy level?

The practice this week is threefold.

1. **Lighten up**: Notice and reflect in your journal the things that you take *way too seriously* and what happens when you consciously stop investing "serious" energy in them.

2. **Observe and feel**: As you go about your day, notice what hanging around negative and pessimistic people feels like and what it does specifically to your energy level. Notice, in contrast, what it feels like to surround yourself with positive, optimistic people and what that does to your energy level.

3. **Let 'er rip!** Whatever makes you smile, laugh out loud, guffaw, or split a seam, give yourself permission to read it, watch it, listen to it, cultivate it. Sneak it in if you have to. Every day. Notice what happens when you start to replace the more

sluggish energy of seriousness with the lighter frequencies of joy.

Journal Revealings

◇ Encounters that I've had that make no sense and perfect sense at the same time . . .

◇ Things about myself that I take way too seriously . . .

◇ What "serious" feels like when I tune in to it as a form of energy (and what "joy" feels like in comparison) . . .

◇ When I'm around negative, pessimistic Debbie Downers I feel . . . (and what it does specifically to my energy level is . . .)

◇ When I'm around positive, upbeat, and optimistic people I feel . . . (and what doing so does specifically to my energy level is . . .)

◇ What makes me laugh out loud (and ways I can cultivate more of it) . . .

Claim Your Worth

You are the truth from foot to brow.
Now, what else would you like to know?
— Rumi, translated by Coleman Barks

How do I make a difference? Why do I matter? *How* do I matter?

Does it even matter?

Thought leader and blogger Seth Godin had me thinking deeply about these questions long after I'd read and bookmarked his post from years ago called "You Matter." As he put it,

> When you love the work you do and the people you do it with, you matter. . . .
>
> When you leave the world a better place than you found it, you matter. . . .
>
> When you touch the people in your life through your actions (and your words), you matter. . . .
>
> When the room brightens when you walk in, you matter.
>
> And when the legacy you leave behind lasts for hours, days or a lifetime, you matter.

I had to try it myself. My personal inquiry led to these free-associated variations of how I matter:

◇ When I put people at ease, I matter.

◇ When I laugh at my own quirks and flaws, I matter.

◇ When I can let others blow off steam without taking it, or them, personally, I matter.

◇ When I can allow myself to make a mistake without beating myself up, I matter.

◇ When I can say no (even if it makes me cringe with discomfort), I matter.

◇ When I speak from the heart, I matter. (And even when I can't manage it, I matter too.)

◇ When I notice the energy in the room brightening simply by showing up and being present, I know I matter.

And if I forget, all I need to do is reach for this pearl of wisdom by Hafiz:

This place where you are right now
God circled on a map for you.

Your turn. What would you like to say to name and claim your worth?

Practice

Why do you matter? How do you matter?

The practice this week is to remember why you matter. Sit comfortably, take a deep breath, and free-associate your own list in your journal that names and claims your worth. Notice what this download feels like before, during, and after. Take the feelings into your day and notice any shifts in how people respond to you.

Journal Revealings

◇ Why I matter . . .

◇ How I matter . . .

◇ What it feels like to remember that I matter . . .

WEEK 50

Shine and Thrive

Around me the trees stir in their leaves
and call out, "Stay awhile."
The light flows from their branches.

And they call again, "It's simple," they say,
"and you too have come into the world
to do this, to go easy, to be filled
with light, and to shine."
—Mary Oliver

How big do you want to be? How much can you handle?

What I mean by that is, how *spacious* do you want to be, and how much *light* are you willing to allow in and receive?

These questions came to me recently in a conversation I had with my husband about aging and the fears that come with it, as in the thought of time running out before we've fully realized our true potential or done everything we came here to do.

Even the word "retire" sounds so . . . um . . . *tired.* It feels tight and contracted. It has no energy or life force.

You see, my husband and I don't think of ourselves as ever retiring in the classic sense—or "getting old," for that matter. While the body's creaks and groans might indicate otherwise, we believe that there is no reason to ever stop growing and evolving. As long as we continue to dissolve limiting beliefs, patterns, and habits and choose to embrace vitality, mystery, and wonder, there's no telling what blessings are yet to be revealed.

So why limit ourselves? As we shine more brightly, so too will the higher frequencies of light, new opportunities, and fresh experiences that we attract. It's an immutable law of physics. Besides, as Marianne Williamson so famously wrote in *A Return to Love*:

> Your playing small doesn't serve the world. There's nothing enlightened about shrinking so that other people won't feel insecure around you. We are all meant to shine, as children do. . . . And as we let our own light

shine, we unconsciously give other people permission to do the same.

I'd like to think that after fifty weeks on this journey you're experiencing more of the goodies that come from being willing to play a bigger game: new awarenesses, synchronicities and pleasant surprises, greater ease, shifts in perception, more bandwidth, more beauty, more time, more light, more love.

Even if you don't feel quite there yet in the spacious department, it might help to remember the spiral staircase analogy from Week 20.

It's all good. It all matters. Everything that preceded this moment has informed and grown you. You are not the same person you were fifty weeks ago, no matter how bad things may seem sometimes, no matter what your mind tells you . . .

You have changed.

Yes, there will always be those days when you feel really small, contracted, and you can't see past your nose. That would be the time to remember Adrienne Maree Brown's message from Week 20: "Things are not getting worse, they are getting uncovered." Or, to repeat our mantra from Week 44, inspired by Dr. Emile Coué, "Every day, in every way, I am getting better and better."

That would also be the time to reach for the five S's and take heart—literally. The work of growing your spacious muscle begins with consistent and compassionate acts of kindness for yourself.

No matter how many times you've circled around the sun in this lifetime, there are many compelling reasons to be hopeful and excited about the years ahead.

As we close the chapter on the fifth and final step to spaciousness—self-care—I can't think of a better way to celebrate this fifty-week milestone than to circle back and reflect on how far we've come, both in this book and in our lives, and allow it to move us forward . . .

Beginning with opening up the letter you wrote to your future self back in Week 1. Remember it?

You may recall that you were asked to write a letter, sign it, put it in an envelope, and seal it to open at a later date. Well that date is now. Today is your day to open that letter and read what you wrote to yourself almost a year ago.

Big or small, subtle or sublime, shifts in perception or surprise encounters, waking dreams or symbols, magic moments or holy moments, miracles or connections with something larger than yourself—whatever points to changes you've experienced this year, give yourself some space to reflect upon it in your journal and receive its blessings.

You are definitely not the same person you were when you began this journey. You are way more, way bigger than that!

Practice

In what ways have you grown and changed over the course of this year? In what ways have you turned up the light and grown more spacious? What can you do to support yourself going forward?

Give yourself plenty of time this week to reflect in your journal how far you've come this year. The threefold practice this week will help you.

1. **Read your letter**: Find a quiet place to sit, make yourself a cup of tea, get comfy, and read the letter you wrote a year ago to your future self. After you've read it once, read it a second time and think about what moves you about this letter. In what ways have you changed? In what ways have you surprised yourself? In what ways have you cultivated the things that you most desired back then (or not quite)? What new hopes and goals could use your support going forward?

2. **Review and highlight**: Go through your journal and mark the sections that have been the biggest revelations so far for you.

3. **Write a letter to your younger self**: Express gratitude and appreciation to yourself for the hard work you did to get where you are now, and the wisdom you've gained because of it. Tell yourself some of the ways you've turned up your light and what you're looking forward to experiencing in the years ahead.

Journal Revealings

◇ What has been most revealing to me about this year . . .

◇ What moves me most about reading my letter to my future self . . .

◇ Ways that I have changed this year or surprised myself . . .

◇ Goals I set for myself that I was able to cultivate or achieve . . .

◇ Goals that still need my love and attention . . .

◇ Ways that I can support myself going forward . . .

◇ Dear younger self, thank you for . . .

PART 6

COMING HOME

*I also allowed my life to be guided by a strange
language, which I call "signs." I know the world is
talking to me, and I need to listen to it, and if I do
that, I will always be guided toward what there is of
the most intense, passionate and beautiful.*
—Paulo Coelho

If you were to look back on your life, what are some of the ways
your soul has nudged and steered you? In what ways do you
feel that the Universe has your back? What would you like to
remember about this year that you can take with you into your
daily life as you go forward?

Let's home in.

In the last two weeks of our journey together, we will connect some dots and shine light on the path going forward.

Dream and Beam

No one expected me. Everything awaited me.
—Patti Smith

In 2004 my husband and I did a crazy thing. We bought a ruin in central Mexico. The idea was to build a modest home there that would give us a little getaway. Even back then, when this town had not yet been discovered and declared a UNESCO World Heritage site, the cost of the land was beyond our means. We had to scrape together everything we had to make it happen.

The one-story property had been abandoned for years. There was junk and trash strewn everywhere. The walls of the kitchen were covered in soot from years of open-fire cooking. The ceilings were teeming with scorpions (we later learned).

After signing the papers, our young, unknown, and inexpensive architect-builder informed us that there was no guarantee that we'd receive the necessary permits from the town's historic commission to build a second floor, nor a guarantee of reasonable views from the rooftop if we got those permissions. What started out as doable and exciting began to look more hopeless by the minute; a lost cause, a massive mistake.

Had we gone mad? What were we thinking? What was it that got us to lose our minds so completely and utterly over a certified *dump*?

The answer: a little tree.

Yes, what grabbed our hearts, pulled us in, and wouldn't let go was a single, thriving pomegranate tree that had survived years of neglect. There she stood like a sentry in the middle of the chaos, waiting, it seemed, for us to cross the threshold and become the next stewards of the place.

That tree was a slice of heaven, an invitation, a promise of something nourishing and good.

And like any good host, this tree welcomed us on the day of the closing with bushels of fruit—real ones and virtual ones—that would soon become a bounty of spacious reveals that would surpass our wildest hopes and imaginings.

In the end, we were able to secure the permits that allowed us to add a second story and transform the property into a cozy sanctuary of patios, plantings, and fountains—all within a period of a few months. Our builder might have been young, hungry, and inexperienced, but he was very good and *fast*.

The project was a feast for the senses, an unfolding palette of living art, a magic playground of possibility and beauty. It awakened in me a passion I'd had since I was a child and had long forgotten, which was a deep love for creating beautiful home spaces that nourish and support people.

And if that were not expansive enough, the experience of pouring our love into this place was topped off with the most unexpected gift of all: rooftop access to exquisite 360-degree views that went on for miles. We were living on top of the world.

Ten months after jumping off the cliff into this crazy idea, we celebrated Christmas in our sparkling new casita. We named her Casita del Granado, or Little House of the Pomegranate Tree. She is the boss, after all—the divine space holder of this heavenly home.

As we turn the corner on our year together, I invite you to use this week to explore some of the whispery or loud ways your soul has nudged and steered you in the direction of a life purpose, personal dream, or unexpected adventure, and some of the ways you knowingly or unknowingly listened to these nudges, pushed through resistance, and followed through.

No matter how successful you were in the end, how wonderful or horrible the outcome, what I'm really interested in are the goodies that you received from the experience itself, the gifts that come from hanging out in the messy middle where nothing is certain and nothing is ever assured, as social scientist and writer Rosabeth Moss Kanter suggests here:

> Welcome to the miserable middles of change. This is the time when Kanter's Law kicks in. Everything looks like a failure in the middle. Everyone loves inspiring beginnings and happy endings; it is just the middles that involve hard work.

Yes, that is what I'm interested in.

Practice

If you were to look back into your past, what signs did you heed that might have looked bad or confusing on paper and ended up being pivotal, or even game-changing? In what ways did you choose not-knowing over comfort, and what helped you keep going?

The practice this week is to go back in time: use the spacious awareness process below to connect some dots that might help you answer these questions and give you more clarity about your abilities to realize your deepest dreams. Use the journal prompts to go deeper.

Spacious Awareness Process

This process can be done as a visualization or as a reflective writing exercise in your journal. Either way, before you begin, please review and follow the opening guidelines and centering process (Step 1) from the Practice in Week 28.

1. **Get centered**: Get comfortable, and take an easy breath in and a slow, emptying breath out. Connect with how you are feeling right now by doing a quick sensory body scan. Keep breathing in and out as you become even more relaxed . . . and present . . . and still . . .

2. **Recall**: Reflect on a time in your life when you followed an impulse, or a nudge, or call to adventure to do something that offered no promise of success

or reward. It could have been a big life change like leaving a job or spouse, moving to another part of the country or the world, or making a major investment of money or time. It could have been something small and seemingly insignificant at the time, like taking a class, going on a blind date, clearing out some clutter, or choosing to go left instead of right. Try to go with your first thought and don't think too hard. Once you have it, allow yourself to be guided to connect with the experience via the following questions:

◇ What did the nudge feel like? Use all of your senses to tune in to both the excitement and the fears that you experienced. Was this impulse loud, making you feel giddy, like, *Wow this could be really awesome . . . I would love to do that (have that, be that)?* Or was the impulse more quiet and whispery—just enough to tickle your curiosity and get your attention? Are you aware of any fear mixed in with the sparks of curiosity that might have given you pause or made you feel queasy? Were you terrified? If so, what did that feel like?

◇ What did the signs or whisperings look like? Whether overt or internal, what was it exactly that got you to pay attention and move ahead with your choice?

◊ What blocks or resistances did you have to overcome and what steps did you take to support yourself, if at all? Did you ask someone to help you?

◊ Looking back on the situation, what was the gift? What did you gain from the experience? In what ways did the outcome exceed your expectations, or fall short?

◊ In what ways do you feel that the Universe has your back? In what ways do you feel that your honoring of this call to adventure played out perfectly, that all of it was as it should be, and there really are no mistakes?

3. **Release**: Take any lingering issues, unresolved feelings, or painful memories that you may still be carrying and release them with love. They served their purpose to perfection, and now it is safe to let them go.

4. **Express gratitude**: Bring your awareness to your heart. Thank it for its infinite wisdom and all the ways that it has served and supported you unconditionally throughout your life. Ask that it deliver continued clarity, guidance, and direction—in

ways that you will recognize and can easily integrate going forward.

5. **Tune in**: Take another nice, deep breath in and a slow, emptying breath out. And just notice how your body is feeling now. How's your energy level? How about your breathing? Do you feel the same now or different than when you began this process? Bring your awareness back to yourself sitting in the room and reach for a tall glass of water.

6. **Journal**: Use the prompts that follow to write down your insights and deepen your experience of this process.

Journal Revealings

◇ An impulse that I heeded . . .

◇ When I tune in to the excitement and the fears with all of my senses, it felt . . .

◇ Signs (overt or internal) that got me to pay attention in the first place and/or kept me going . . .

◇ Ways that I (knowingly or unknowingly) moved through resistance and advocated for myself . . .

◇ The gifts this experience gave me . . .

◇ Ways that my heart has never led me astray and what I can do to remember to ask for and listen to its guidance going forward . . .

◇ Ways that I know the Universe has my back, it's all perfect timing, and there are really no mistakes . . .

WEEK 52

Happy New You!

And we are put on earth a little space,
That we may learn to bear the beams of love
—William Blake

Congratulations for going on this ride with me and taking this year for you! Whether you feel that much has changed in your life or not, you have done the most important thing: given yourself this gift of spaciousness.

Perhaps you'll recall what I wrote back in the Introduction about taking a yearlong adventure. Here it is again in case you've forgotten:

The truth is, most people rarely set out, purposefully, to spend 365 days doing something nourishing—something just for themselves—with a commitment to mark the changes that arise in their lives. We don't know how powerful we can be, transforming our lives, taking care of ourselves, one day at a time, over an extended time. . .

And unless we go on the journey and stick with it, we cannot fully know what our higher self wants to teach us.

Well, now you can say that you've done it—or at least that you gave it your best shot—not knowing what you would experience. It takes courage, discipline, and heart to stick with something this long.

So how does it feel to have traveled the distance?

Whether or not you feel you've poured your whole heart into this experience or not, or put as much into your clearing as you'd hoped and journaled about it, it's okay. Remember, this is a journey. Journeys don't end. They never end.

They get better.

Going forward, you can start again from the beginning, if it moves you, or pick up where you left off, or open the book randomly each day or week and play with its message. The material may be the same, but you won't be. (Remember the spiral staircase?)

As my graduation gift to you, I would like to honor our year together by looking back and looking forward:

As a way of looking back, I made a three-minute video featuring some of my favorite images that inspired the writing of this book. When I talked in Week 43 about going off-road and making art, this is it: a small culling of photographs I took that year that helped me find myself again. You'll recognize the photographs I reference in my stories. With a few exceptions, each slide matches the theme and message of each chapter of this book, including a short sequence of the shirtless bike rider wearing a crazy hat, flying a kite, and playing a trumpet that I write about in Week 48. The video is called "Happy New You!" and you can find it in the Resources section of this book. May these images fill you up, beam you out, and inspire you to keep going in your clearing practice.

In the spirit of remembering, continuing the journey, and looking forward, I offer you six touchstones and a blessing to inspire you as well. Keep them close by, or post them somewhere where you'll see them often. May they remind you to . . .

1. **Take your time**: Remember to go slow so you don't "miss the show."

2. **Dial it back**: Remember that reducing stress and overwhelm is instantly possible when you stop, breathe, and simplify.

3. **Come to your senses**: Remember that life is more rich, enlivening, and illuminating when you allow yourself to feel and follow your "knows."

4. **Be the witness**: Remember that being a compassionate observer frees you. It makes you be more available to respond with equanimity in any

situation. It gives you more SPACE, more flow, and a clearer view.

5. **Honor your process**: Remember that everyone wins when you love yourself, claim your worth, and expand your capacity to receive.

6. **Realize your dreams**: May you shine your light brightly, and may your deepest desires be realized in delightful, unexpected, and recognizable ways.

Yes, that is what I wish for all of us going forward.

And as the famous essayist and humorist Mark Twain once said:

Twenty years from now, you will be more disappointed by the things you didn't do than by the ones that you did. So throw off the bowlines. Sail away from the safe harbor. Catch the trade winds in your sails. Explore. Dream. Discover.

I wish you happy travels!

Keep beaming, my friends. I'll see you on the path.

Practice

If you could have another year just for you, what would that look like?

Use this week to set your intentions and make a plan for a Year Two Clear! It could be a return to the beginning of this book or a different journey. In the back of this book, under Next Steps, you'll find additional ideas and opportunities to help you keep rolling and growing with your clearing.

Journal Revealings

◇ What I most desire to cultivate for myself as I continue forward . . .

◇ Specific steps I can take to make that happen . . .

ACKNOWLEDGMENTS

It takes a village. To all the beings who have nurtured and fueled me to do what I love, helped me grow as a teacher, supported me in getting my message out into the world, kept me going when I felt lost and didn't know what I was doing . . . let me just say right out of the gate: *A Year for You* would not exist without you!

A Year for You wouldn't exist either without its two older siblings: *Your Spacious Self* and *A Year to Clear*. From foundation to journey to practice, I love how this material as grown organically over the years, each book playing an important role in the Spacious Way of things.

To my publisher, Randy Davila: I didn't know I even had one book in me, let alone three! Thank you again for your continued belief in my work. Your masterful direction, generous support, and guiding friendship mean the world. As we all know everything needs a home. Thank you for giving the Spacious Way series a beautiful place at Hierophant Publishing to call home.

To Addie Talbot and Allison McDaniel: thank you for nudging me to dig deeper in the first round of edits, for helping me to bring out the very best of this project. And Susie Pitzen:

there is no one who appreciates a thorough editorial "space clearing" more than I! Thank you for smoothing out all the rough edges and upleveling the content to make this book spark and sparkle with joy! Emma Smith: I'll have one of those bathrooms with the sweeping views! Seriously, you nailed it with this book's beautiful cover that feels so inviting, nourishing, and expansive. Thank you.

To all my readers of *A Year to Clear* and students of "A Year to Clear What's Holding You Back!" who said *YES!* to a yearlong clearing adventure: thank you for your trust in me. The courage, vulnerability, and joyful reveals that pour through your stories and comments (tens of thousands of them) inspire me daily. Your willingness to show up every day and hang out in the "messy middle" with awareness and compassion inspires us all to hang out in ours. If you ever doubt how powerful you are individually and collectively, consider this: *A Year for You* was inspired largely by you.

To readers and students whose personal stories grace these pages: thank you for sharing your vulnerabilities, moving us with your creative ideas, and touching us with your heart. It is stories like yours that give us hope and keep us going. They help us come out of our respective cluttered "closets" and heal the patterns that got us there.

To Marcus Buckingham, Elizabeth Gilbert, Seth Godin, Anne Lamott, Marie Kondo, Tyler Lewke, Jacob Nordby, Julie Peters, Eckhart Tolle, Elizabeth Watt, and other fellow writers, teachers, and thought leaders whose inspiring voices appear in this book: thank you for doing what you do every day to enlighten and elevate us.

To my family—my heart, *mi vida*: I love you more than words can say. Thank you, Camilla, for letting me share your story that can help us heal from heartbreak and embrace loss. Your courage, resilience, and willingness to pick yourself up—again and again—in the face of disappointing setbacks is breathtaking—and so is your ability to problem solve and think on your feet! I'll always remember the breakthrough moment (for me) of sitting at that beach house stewing over how to work in the concept of a "letter to your future self": how quickly you stepped in, cut right through the noise and, in less than two minutes, crafted the most artful approach. It is moments like these—of watching you step into your power as a young woman—that make me so very hopeful for our future and proud to be your mama.

And Jay—my beloved, devoted partner, best friend, confidant, ally, advocate, master planner, co-mischief-maker and world traveler: thank you for saying *YES!* to me over thirty-five years ago and joining me on this journey of a lifetime. Here's to many more "sail ins," sunset "shows," and spacious adventures that make us feel young and keep us laughing.

Finally, in the words of Baba Ram Dass who said: "We are all just walking each other home," *thank you all* for your part in walking me home!

RESOURCES BY CHAPTER

Introduction

Stephanie Bennett Vogt. *Your Spacious Self: Clear the Clutter and Discover Who You Are* (San Antonio, TX: Hierophant Publishing, 2012).

Stephanie Bennett Vogt. *A Year to Clear: A Daily Guide to Creating Spaciousness in Your Home and Heart* (San Antonio, TX: Hierophant Publishing, 2015).

Week 1

Pico Iyer, "Want to Be Happy? Slow Down." *Ideas.TED.com*, http://ideas.ted.com/want-to-be-happy-slow-down/.

Seth Godin, "Transformation Tourism." *Seth's Blog,* http://sethgodin.typepad.com/seths_blog/2016/04/transformation-tourism.html.

Week 10

"Have You Ever Heard Crickets Chirping Slowed Down? Its Amazing!" Soul Seekers, https://youtu.be/UqU5OMNL-7I.

Week 14

"The Importance of Making Your Bed—US Navy Admiral William H. McRaven." *Business Insider,* https://youtu.be/GKZRFDCbGTA?t=1s.

Week 16

"Marie Kondo: Basic Folding Method." *Ebury Reads*, https://
youtu.be/Lpc5_1896ro.

Weeks 12, 16, and 17

Marie Kondo. *The Life-Changing Magic of Tidying Up: The Japanese
Art of Decluttering and Organizing* (Berkeley, CA: Ten Speed Press,
2014).

Week 22

Elizabeth Watt. "The Good Eye," *Elizabeth Watt,* https://eliza-
bethwatt.com/the-good-eye/.

Elizabeth Watt. "Beauty Everywhere," *Elizabeth Watt,* https://
elizabethwatt.com/beauty-everywhere/.

Week 25

"Chef's Table Official Trailer." Netflix, https://www.youtube.
com/embed/qKqj85oo2wI.

Week 27

Soundscapes to help quiet noise, sleep, calm down, relax,
https://mynoise.net/.

Week 28

Julie Peters, "Feeling Bad About Feeling Bad: Shame and the
Primal Brain," *Spirituality & Health*, https://spiritualityhealth.
com/blogs/downward-blog-a-life-in-yoga/2017/09/14/feeling-
bad-about-feeling-bad-shame-and-the-primal-brain.

Week 30

"Murmuration." Islands and Rivers, https://vimeo.com/31158841.

Week 35

"Get Out of the Materialism Trap Now," Erin Janus, https://youtu.be/Qk1i7UGBz1Q.

Week 37

"Children interrupt BBC News Interview," *BBC News,* https://youtu.be/Mh4f9AYRCZY.

Week 38

Eckhart Tolle, *A New Earth: Awakening to Your Life's Purpose* (New York: Penguin Books, 2016).

Week 39

Dan Brown, *The Da Vinci Code* (New York: Random House, 2003).

Week 42

Tyler Lewke, "An Addict's Version of Self-Care." *Posts from the Path*, http://postsfromthepath.com/sustainable-happiness/an-addicts-version-of-self-care.html.

Karen Bouris with Anne Lamott, "Life as a Black-Belt Codependent," *Spirituality & Health,* https://spiritualityhealth.com/articles/2012/12/13/anne-lamott-life-black-belt-codependent.

Week 43

Marcus Buckingham, *Find Your Strongest Life: What The Happiest and Most Successful Women Do Differently* (Nashville, TN: Thomas Nelson, 2009).

Week 44

Elizabeth Gilbert, *Big Magic: Creative Living Beyond Fear* (New York: Riverhead Books, 2015).

Week 46

Elizabeth Gilbert, "My Tiny Writing Room." *Facebook,* June 13, 2018, https://www.facebook.com/GilbertLiz/posts/1859400414142065.

Melissa Camara Wilkins, "10 Things Minimalists Don't Do." *No Sidebar,* http://nosidebar.com/things-minimalists-dont-do/.

Week 49

Seth Godin, "You Matter." *Seth's Blog,* https://seths.blog/2009/06/you-matter/.

Week 51

Rosabeth Moss Kanter, "Change is Hardest in the Middle." *Harvard Business Review,* https://hbr.org/2009/08/change-is-hardest-in-the-middl.

Week 52

Stephanie Bennett Vogt, "Happy New You!" (aka "My Year For Me: A Photographic Journey"), https://youtu.be/rsreTd0umac.

NEXT STEPS

Want more? Here are some additional resources from Stephanie to support and inspire a clear home and a spacious life:

A Year to Clear What's Holding You Back!
A 365-day online course by Stephanie Bennett Vogt; www.dailyom.com.

Clearing Physical and Emotional Clutter
A 365-day online course by Stephanie Bennett Vogt; www.dailyom.com.

Clear Your Home, Clear Your Life
A 28-day online course by Stephanie Bennett Vogt; www.dailyom.com.

A Year to Simplify Your Life
A 52-week online course by Stephanie Bennett Vogt; www.dailyom.com.

Light Reveals: Finding Beauty and Magic in the Every Day
Spacious images by Stephanie Bennett Vogt; www.instagram.com/spaciousway/.

SpaceClear: Home to Your Spacious Self
The online home for all of Stephanie Bennett Vogt's resources to cultivate a clear home and spacious life; www.spaceclear.com.

AUTHOR'S NOTE

Thank you for your willingness to give yourself this nourishing gift of a year. May your spacious self continue to flourish and reveal itself in wonderous ways.

It takes a village of "spacious s-elves" to build a clearing movement. If you have received value from this book, I invite you to spread the word. Share a success story or a testimonial on Amazon or Goodreads—whatever moves you to inspire hope, encourage others, and help create the spacious energy that can lighten the load for others and change the world.

ABOUT THE AUTHOR

Stephanie Bennett Vogt is a teacher, space clearing expert, and the author of *Your Spacious Self: Clear the Clutter and Discover Who You Are* and *A Year to Clear: A Daily Guide to Creating Spaciousness in Your Home and Heart.* She brings forty years of teaching experience to SpaceClear, the practice she founded in 1996 to help homes and people come into balance.

Stephanie has taught her inspirational clearing programs at centers worldwide, including the Kripalu Center for Yoga & Health and the New England School of Feng Shui, and is the creator of four best-selling courses, offered on DailyOM, which have attracted nearly 200,000 participants.

Stephanie and her husband divide their time between Concord, Massachusetts, and San Miguel de Allende, Mexico.

Visit her at www.spaceclear.com.

Hierophant Publishing
books that inspire your body, mind, and spirit

Hierophant Publishing
8301 Broadway, Suite 219
San Antonio, TX 78209
888-800-4240

www.hierophantpublishing.com